Relationship

Needs, Framework, and Models

Enhanced Edition

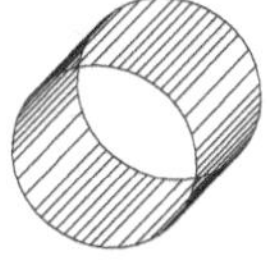

Author’s Books

(As of June 20, 2020)*

Non-fiction

The Nature of Love and Relationships 2011, **2016**
Doubts and Decisions for Living:
Volume I: The Foundation of Human Thoughts **2014**
Volume II: The Sanctity of Human Spirit **2014**
Volume III: The Structure of Human Life **2014**
Relationship Facts, Trends, and Choices **2016**
The Mysteries of Life, Love, and Happiness **2016**
Marriage and Divorce Hardships **2016**
Gender Qualities, Quirks, and Quarrels **2016**
Relationship Needs, Framework, and Models **2016**
Being Better Beings **2020**

Fiction

Persian Moons 2007, **2016**
Midnight Gate-opener 2011, **2016**
My Lousy Life Stories **2014**
Persian Suns **2021 (Planned)**

---

* 12 older books are Enhanced Editions and printed in 2020. They were resubmitted to the Library and Archives Canada Cataloguing as well. If a book's ‘print date’ on the copyright page is older, the newest version is available at Amazon and bookstores.

Love and Relationships Series
5

Relationship

Needs, Framework, and Models

(Guidelines for Success)

Tom Omidi, Ph.D.

Omidi, Tom, 1945-
Relationship needs, framework, and models: guidelines for success / Tom Omidi.

(Love and relationships series ; 5)
ISBN 978-1-988351-08-7 (paperback)

1. Interpersonal relations. 2. Man-woman relationships. 3. Interpersonal communication. 4. Communication in marriage. 5. Interpersonal conflict. 6. Marital conflict. 7. Conflict management. 8. Couples Psychology. 9. Married people Psychology. I. Title.

Old edition at
Library and Archives Canada Cataloguing in Publication
HQ801.O455 2016 306.8 C2016-902408-3

Published by Eros Books,
Vancouver, British Columbia
Canada

erosbooks2020.@gmail.com

Enhanced and Printed in 2020

Table of Contents

Table of Contents (Cont.)

List of Diagrams and Tables

Introduction

The speedy social evolution in recent decades has changed the nature and format of family relationships quite carelessly to the point where now society itself is threatened by the poor health of relationships. The accelerating marital conflicts are largely responsible for the growing social stress, which in turn disturbs the whole socioeconomic structure, too. The question is how societies can survive if relationships keep distressing the population and causing so much havoc.

Nobody deserves the agonies of marriage breakdown and loneliness. Yet, our own ignorance about relationships' unique needs must be blamed for the present conundrums. Ultimately, we are responsible for our pains due to our flimsy mentalities towards marriage. Nonetheless, marital hassles rendering such dire personal and social dilemmas make the mission of finding lasting solutions quite urgent and sacred.

At two extremes, 'companionship' feels like a spiritual connection or a boring obligation between partners. We may perceive relationships as a divine experience in beauty and selflessness, or merely a means of self-gratification and social adaptation. While the latter position appears closer to reality, the former reflects our instinctual search for perfection and spirituality. In modern societies, people's romantic perceptions of relationships cover both of these extremes and everything else between them. Especially, more people strive, nowadays, to find their soul mates to share love, yet remain incapable of managing their relationships realistically. While partners' inner conflicts heighten due to their sense of failure to satisfy their needs for reliable mates, they have no clear understanding of relationships' unique needs and their roles in fulfilling them.

The reason is that social changes have been too drastic and misleading. They have tainted our personalities, perceptions of the world, and expectations from life. We have become too spoiled, needy, and impatient. In fact, we have lost our senses about relationships' real purposes and their capacity to handle so many of our deep insecurities. Meanwhile, our relentless search for a reliable companion, often with hurtful experiences and outcomes, raises our stress and confusion.

Sadly, we seem helpless to create a proper balance between practicality and romance. We often fail to use commonsense when it is wise to be practical, and we do not know how or when to express emotions when it can sweeten a relationship. For example, most people have felt that signing a prenuptial agreement is necessary as a practical measure, but doing so still appears businesslike and unromantic. We like to believe that relationships should begin with romance and trust. Our need for a companion is so strong we just commit ourselves prematurely and set high expectations for the success of our relationships, too. Ironically, most of us keep thinking all along about the financial risks of our relationships privately. These days, especially, we are too calculating and businesslike about relationships. Yet, we shyly (or slyly) hide those unromantic thoughts, to ease into a relationship in hopes of soothing our mental burdens and insecurities. Deliberately and naively, we ignore the high possibility of separation and all the added pain that relationships usually bring to couples' lives, anyway. The truth is that our *urgent* emotional *needs* (e.g., need for sex and attention) overpower our ability to think practically about the potential hardships of relationships. This happens a lot, since our spirits are usually weakened by other harsh realities of modern lifestyles. We have become too soft and lonely. We also believe that luring in a companion needs romance, which should not be contaminated with matters of practicality. Only afterwards, we become logical (calculating) in running our relationships, while losing sight of all the romance we had felt before. However, all evidences about relationship calamities indicate that we must be doing exactly the opposite, i.e., to be practical first and romantic later.

Obviously, tainted family and social norms are responsible for marital failures, which damage social morale and ethics extensively in return. The only way out of this vicious cycle is to review our convoluted vision of relationships and reset it slowly to elude further social decline. Our *personal mentality* has to change in order to fit our newer social structure. The *social mentality* regarding relationships and the government's role should also be modified so that people can deal with the complex nature of modern relationships *more personally* and seriously. We need a progressive legal system in line with people's new approach to relationships, but less government interference. Only then, a less hectic relationship environment would gradually reduce the burdens on societies and people. The required deep changes in people and social mentalities are discussed throughout this book. Government's responsibilities and role are discussed briefly in Chapter Eleven as well. Only with these personal and social changes, we might reverse the fast deteriorating fate of relationships.

Of course, some relationships thrive merely on the strength of partners' mature personalities. Sometimes, one partner is enlightened enough to make their marriage flourish all alone. Sometimes, one enlightened partner can bring out the good in his/her partner, too. And, of course, sometimes, he/she faces the harshest resistance by his/her partner and actually receives malice against his/her good intentions. Anyway, the number of relationships flourishing due to partners' goodness is miniscule. Thus, this book's goal is to suggest long-terms solutions useful for the large majority of relationships in the new era. Overall, a mental overhaul at global level seems urgent.

Although many of the suggestions made in this book are partly futuristic in terms of radical changes required in both people's attitudes and social mechanisms, they offer enough guidelines to improve our relationships right away and benefit from simple routines that can help develop a more tranquil and cooperative relationship setting. We are capable of changing our mentalities gradually, but even small adjustments could make major impacts on the health of our relationships, while we should also push our leaders and governments to consider the fundamental (and rather radical) ideas suggested in this book for revamping social mechanisms.

Some of the theories and suggestions in this book might appear somewhat technical for people to grasp right away, but with some focus and patience, they can understand and put them into practice. Mostly, however, it is hoped that family experts and marriage counsellors can help people with these concepts as necessary. Our universities should also take on the crucial task of finding realistic solutions about relationships along with innovative legal mechanisms that governments could implement to help relationships' dwindling situation in the modern world. Then, of course, the biggest challenge is to propagate the concepts of relationship needs, framework, and models within our modern culture.

PART I

Relationship Needs

Chapter One

Relationships Environment

We consider older cultures outmoded mainly in terms of women's demoted status. Obviously, inequality and abuse are intolerable. However, our modern approaches are proving even more unproductive. The stress of new lifestyles is crippling a good majority of relationships and threatening the foundation of our societies. The situation is only going to worsen if good solutions and a framework for relationships are not found soon and people do not become wiser about their needs.

A major source of marital failures is that couples perceive and define their 'relationship needs'[†] as an extension of their personal needs. Most of us assume that personal needs and relationship needs are the same, or they should coincide. Some people are even more selfish and insist that their needs must supersede their partners' and any possible *relationship needs*. They try to dominate their partners and set crooked guidelines for their relationships. All along, we assume that relationships' main (and often 'only') goal is to make us happy. We expect to find a reliable spouse who is not only waiting for us out there, but also very capable of bringing us love and happiness automatically.

[†] The two terms 'Relationship Needs' and 'Relationships' Needs' are used interchangeably in this book to imply the generic needs of all relationships.

We have no logical sense about the nature of relationships in the new era. Instead, we naively trust our perceptions and assumptions, which have gradually grown around our shallow observations and interpretations. We have embraced immense misperceptions about love and happiness all along, which have overwhelmed and paralysed our lives and relationships. Meanwhile, our rising neediness for things and compassion puts extra pressures on relationships. We have developed a huge amount of superficial needs, in recent decades, over and above our already abused instinctual needs, such as sexuality. Meanwhile, society propagates crooked values and behaviour, including individualism, that goad us become too demanding and arrogant. This trend is accelerating in line with people's tendency to imitate others and adopt consumerism too eagerly. Therefore, not only we see relationship needs as an extension of our personal needs, but also make many odd assumptions about the purpose of relationships and our partner's ability and duty to fulfil our expectations.

Thus, while struggling with our neediness, misperceptions, and partners' demands, we never give ourselves a chance to perform some self-analysis and raise our self-awareness and self-reliance for pursuing a practical existence either within or outside a marriage. We get little time, interest, and patience to assess the purposes of our lives and personal habits. Instead, we let our inflated personal needs and imaginations numb our capacity to envision a practical meaning and purpose for our relationships. We ignore that now relationships have their own particular needs that if not understood and satisfied, we would never find peace, but only keep fighting our spouses forever.

Surely, we cannot stop social progress or change people's mentalities and needs that will continue to dictate the kind of relationships they are willing to accept for their preferred type of lifestyle. Accordingly, the meaning, purpose, and format of relationships need regular reassessments and adjustments in line with drastic changes in social trends and values. Yet, so far, we have not had the chance and a mechanism to do so. We have not adapted our relationships to new social values and couples' personal mentalities. Instead, we expect our spouses to figure out and satisfy our needs and make us happy, simply because we have accepted to be in a relationship with them.

Overall, the social havoc, nowadays, is due to the lack of a practical framework for our relationships after the fast changes in relationships' environment in recent decades. Parts II and III of this book will study these growing imbalances and suggest a relationship framework more suitable for the new era. First, however, a deeper understanding of the nature of relationships and our options about this issue is necessary. Ultimately, we have three options:

A. **Continue with the status quo**, hoping that a viable format for relationships would emerge eventually as nature takes its course. Meanwhile, more separations, conflicts, and paranoia would make relationships even more torturous. The outcome would be rather unpredictable, but surely not satisfactory, because the chance for a logical and efficient framework evolving out of this chaos is terribly slim.
B. **Hope that one gender will eventually dominate the other** so that order might return to relationships. Sadly, humans have proven unable to relate to one another and work as a team in the long run, especially the opposite sexes. This is truer, nowadays, with arrogance, greed, and individualism besieging our mentalities and social values. However, the option of one gender taking a superior role in relationships would not work in the end, either. Chaos and equality struggles would keep ruining relationships.
C. **Create and propagate a relationship framework** based on prevalent social mentalities to guide couples run their relationships smoothly and relate rather efficiently. With the rising social complexity, relationships' longevity seems doomed, anyway. Yet, a modern relationship framework

can at least do two things: 1) prepare couples for the high likelihood of relationship failures in the new era, and 2) reduce the level of frictions between couples.

Let us hope the third option would appeal to most of us and we decide to support it actively. Only this option has a chance to bring some level of objectivity back into relationships. In addition, a practical relationship framework may force couples to anticipate, and be mentally prepared for, the sad reality of separation and living independently. Nevertheless, this book advocates the third option, as the author believes it provides the only solution for relationships, while minimizing personal anguish, too. We must change our mindset about relationships in order to bring relative peace into our lives. We should adopt and support some new ideas, although they oppose our present idealism about relationships. This new mentality would help us personally to find our inner self and boost our spirits, while it also proves essential for reversing the deteriorating state of relationships as our social responsibility. As a start, we must learn about the relationships environment, reality, and success factors, as outlined in Part I, to develop a general picture about relationships' generic needs.

To create a framework for relationships, we must think outside the box and adopt some novel ideas that might initially seem too radical and impractical. However, the readers are encouraged to pause and ponder those ideas, as presented in the following pages, while they wait for more justifications and discussions about this framework in Parts II and III. These ideas would make sense if we only try to think realistically and proactively about our options; A, B, and C noted above.

Facts and Trends

Relationship needs must be redefined with time according to the prevailing culture and people's lifestyle choices, as well as their maturity and mentality. Relationships environment has changed drastically in the last few decades. Thus, we must study the facts and trends in the new era to grasp the *current* state of relationships. The following dozen trends provide the gist of the matter, but readers may review nearly 1,000 facts and trends in this author's book, *Relationship Facts, Trends, and Choices*. Overall, we can readily observe that:

1. Nowadays, most people do not look for a partner to satisfy merely their basic companionship need. Rather, they want their relationships make them happy and also satisfy a host of their personal needs or solve their personal problems. Accordingly, they blame their relationships for their failure to figure out life or find happiness on their own.
2. Greed and Ego do not just disappear even when couples happen to be in love. Actually, people's growing drive for individualism and equality would boost their greed and Ego, which in turn reinforce their other pressing needs in relationships, including their needs for control, recognition, identity, love, and retaliation. The point is that love cannot eliminate greed and Ego and all the subsequent problems they create in relationships.
3. People are forced to play games and roles all their lives. They are dragged into situations beyond their control to play along with others and assert themselves. This social condition infects relationships, too, as partners constantly play games and roles—out of necessity, unfortunately. Hardly anybody is natural these days.
4. Couples play games and roles in order to: 1) impress (charm), 2) flatter, 3) intimidate, or 4) snub each other. Therefore, the amount of time they are natural and sincere is small. Accordingly, the level of mistrust in relationships has increased substantially. Discussions in Chapter Two outline some of the reasons for the fast rising mistrust in society and relationships.

5. Personal idiosyncrasies and insecurities have kept growing fast as social values have deteriorated, and vice versa. This vicious cycle would continue to spin out of control and make the success of relationships less likely every year.
6. The probability of finding our soul mate is extremely slim. The probability of finding even a sane, reliable companion has been also diminishing very fast, nowadays. However, we all have difficulty accepting this fact, as we want to stay positive. Our romantic search for a soul mate is preventing us from perceiving relationships realistically and facing life as an independent, self-reliant person.
7. For having a suitable companion (let alone a soul mate), partners must have many common interests and reasonable compatibility, be good humans, understand relationships' unique needs these days, and know how to work on those needs continuously. Yet, human nature does not support all these requirements. In fact, our modern social values make people more arrogant and needy every day, while human nature's impurity increases (and becomes more evident and irritating) with time, too.
8. Most often, partners actually ruin each other's lives, instead of enriching it. This is because life is getting more complex and stressful every year and people have more difficulty coping with social pressures, while they live longer, too. The outcome of this condition is that people have become too disturbed and impatient, nowadays, to deal with their excessive relationship demands effectively.
9. We would always face a major trade off in relationships: They always bring us headaches, whereas for tranquility, we must face loneliness and be self-reliant. The dilemma is to make a right decision according to one's personality.
10. The above facts and hundreds of other reasons explained in this book demonstrate that marriage should be viewed as a temporary arrangement, unless both partners gain all the fine qualities required for building an effective relationship.

11. To attain relative tranquility, we must learn the art of living independently, instead of looking for a soul mate to bring us happiness. For all practical purposes, we must learn to live alone (in the sense of fulfilling our financial and emotional needs personally), instead of seeking relief in relationships.
12. Our only hope is to develop a half dozen or so relationship models that fit couples' varied personalities and needs in line with current culture and couples' mentality. The goal is to provide a relatively tranquil atmosphere for teamwork and effective companionship. This book suggests that only by developing and propagating a relationship framework and its corresponding principles we can achieve this goal. That is the only way to bring some degree of objectivity back into relationships.

Ironically, all couples seem to be on an extensive, torturous training their whole lives mostly through trials and errors and arguments and whining, hoping to find the right processes of communicating, performing family duties, and establishing a practical rapport to run their marriages rather smoothly. At the same time some spouses believe they are experts about all marital issues, and thus their ideas and approaches should be adopted and followed in their relationship, too. Therefore, they try to overrule and dominate their poor spouses a lifetime.

Obviously, neither our lifetime torture to figure out marital secrets and success factors, nor dominating our partners to make our lives easier, are practical and humane. Therefore, we need better mechanisms and mentalities to address modern relationship issues more systematically and objectively for the benefit of the whole society and for the sake of saving so many good marriages that collapse futilely.

The discussions in the following chapters would provide many insights in line with the dozen points made above for handling our relationships more thoughtfully. The objective is to specify relationships' unique needs, which chiefly consist of a set of principles and boundaries to keep partners in harmony and minimize their relationship frictions. The first step for partners would be to understand the perils of their formidable expectations from life and relationships, nowadays, and admit the merits of observing some guidelines in their relationships in line with their modern needs, especially for independence and individualism.

Chapter Two

Relationships Reality

A relationship dies, like any entity, if its needs are ignored. Our lack of knowledge or neglect about these relationships' unique needs by itself explains why so many relationships fail. Now, imagine how shakier and tougher relationships get when partners expect to fulfil their erratic needs in this setting, while their idiosyncrasies and conflicts turn them into mad enemies, instead of loving, happy partners!

Chapters Three and Four explain relationships' needs and sensible expectations that partners can have from their modern marriages. However, first, the gloomy reality of relationships must be pointed out mostly by addressing the effects of our misperceptions or naivety regarding the following seven areas. Understanding the complications that our high expectations and naiveté cause can help refine our mentalities first before exploring the solutions offered in this book:

- Love
- Happiness
- Trust
- Commitment
- Equality
- Human Hormones' Role
- Relationships' Role and Capacity

Love

In the recent decades, couples have suddenly become both too romantic and vastly antagonistic. Everyone believes that love should be the foundation of relationships. In this sense, life has turned into a big theatre. Everybody tries to be romantic. And they expect their partners to be equally good in romance, too, as a test of their commitment. But then they retaliate harshly, and show their evil side, when love fades away—which is a natural event in most relationships. They turn separation into an all-out war when they realize that their supposedly initial love had been a farce. They make life hell for themselves and their partners because love has evaporated (if there had been any real love to begin with). Now couples turn into ferocious adversaries accusing each other of lying about their earlier love promises. They curse their partners for not loving them anymore, as if love were something to force upon oneself and not a natural feeling. They find their partners responsible for the lost love, even if they are the ones feeling out of love. In fact, they often blame their partners for making them fall out of love. They accuse their partners of having killed their love. They also blame them for their loss of youth. The past lovers now suddenly view each other as criminals deserving a severe punishment, including a difficult and costly separation. The penalty for falling out of love is too horrendous, nowadays. Thus, some people keep playing the role of a romantic fool to keep the situation under control. They accept the humiliation of submitting to their spouses' whims to stop their whining, and because the penalties, financially and emotionally, for ending relationships are too high. Nevertheless, most of us feel obliged to be romantic, just to keep up with social norms and expectations. Then again, being romantic is not easy, nor does it prove useful, anyway. Therefore, we just get more confused and sceptical about the nature and purpose of relationships and about our options about our family lives.

Almost everybody finally admits that love, in the way they had initially imagined it, is a transitory state. Then, they may decide that staying in loveless relationships is still preferable to loneliness or high penalties of separation. However, now they do not know how to cope within a relationship that is not defined by love. They believe their relationship has failed and has no value. Some may seek love in another person's arms; to find the love they believe they deserve.

Everybody believes he/she deserves love and must find it somehow. Yet, we all ignore a simple fact about the meaning of love: That the more one seeks selfless love (SLove), the more one must be honest and sincere in character. At the same time, it is becoming harder to be honest, nowadays, due to all the games, especially fake love, introduced in relationships. Of course, we imagine that we can hide our hypocrisy, mistrust, and dishonesty from the rest of the world, which only shows our arrogance and trust in our phony personality (Model) to bail us out. Luckily, people can largely see each other's true nature despite all the silly games they play to portray a false personality of themselves and to hide their calculating nature. In fact, the games and retaliation schemes in relationships show how ridiculous the notion of measuring the strength of our relationships by love is. We just ignore all these contradictions and keep looking for SLove in such a contaminated setting.

Nevertheless, many of us face a big dilemma: On the one hand, getting out of relationships proves excruciating, in terms of the hardships imposed by our partners and the society (the judicial system in particular). On the other hand, many couples are frustrated and confused, nowadays, since they feel trapped in their loveless (usually hostile) relationships. The situation is especially stressful for people who believe love is the essence of relationships. Even worse, many couples must keep playing some phony roles that marriage counsellors tell them to play in order to save their relationships.

Our present mindset reflects our lack of clarity about the nature of love and its role in relationships. Overall, we insist that relationships, and its survival, must be justified and driven by love. In the contemporary definition of relationships, our culture permeates many invalid myths. We believe that:

- Love is the best test of relationships' success.
- Love lasts forever.
- Love makes a relationship last forever.
- Relationships must be validated by love.
- Relationships thrive on love.
- Anybody considering a serious relationship should and would find a person to exchange love with each other.
- Expressing love regularly ensures relationships' success.
- Love is a common phenomenon that everyone grasps and is capable of delivering.
- Love is a common commodity that everyone must find and enjoy in his/her life.
- When there is love, relationship problems are rare and manageable.
- Love overcomes all the relationship problems.
- Partners have control over their feelings to love each other forever.

These myths are furthest from the nature of relationships in the new era. Love does not have the implications or the power stressed in the above myths. Nor do relationships necessarily last longer if partners start theirs mostly with love. We are not learning any lesson from the fact that most relationships in the modern world have started based on *some kind of love* and they still keep failing miserably. It is amazing.

The scientific evidence about the role of human hormones on our behaviour is another proof of our misperception about the power of love. Maybe it is all right to seek love so eagerly. However, we should also remember the flimsy nature of love in general, as well as the chaotic nature of relationships in the new era. We should do so to be prepared for the consequences of our futile search for love or even finding it. We must indeed focus on building our 'self' (selflessness), instead of indulging ourselves with love deficiency and phony lovers. Besides, pure love happens by accident and not active search.

Another cause for misperception in relationships is that partners use love as another yardstick for measuring equality. That is, they expect their partners to love them as much as they think (or pretend) they love their partners. They demand love-equality to ensure the fairness of their relationships. Surely, love-equality is a symptom of the general equality fad in society. People believe that love is a spiritual feeling (Self driven), but then make it totally conditional on their partners' ability to love them equally. Their demands for love equality merely expose their selfishness (instead of selflessness) and destroy their chances to relax and relate naturally.

Couples' perceptions and expressions of love are clearly not unconditional as long as they insist on love equality. It is even more bizarre when they often retaliate harshly when they do not perceive the love they receive adequate. How can this attitude have any trace of spiritual love in it? It is at best only a phoney love (where partners strive to play the role of lovers), without any sense of selflessness (needlessness for equality). This is clearly an example of partners' rising confusion every day regarding their perceptions of love, which leads to more expectations from relationships. The need for general equality has become such an imposing social phenomenon that it has even tainted our love affairs. We are less interested in figuring out how our partners' integrity might qualify them as our soul mates. Nobody knows what the characteristics of a soul mate must be. Rather, we insist on measuring, in greatest accuracy, the equality (as well as the intensity) of the love our partners can show, which we continue to doubt anyway.

Sadly, relationships' chances of survival have declined a lot with love being seen as a main success factor—since love itself cannot survive in relationships. A cynical interpretation of *love* actually implies that it flourishes only by deprivation and not thru a relationship. Maybe believing that relationships (marriage) kill(s) love is cynical. Yet, we can safely say that after the first stages of companionship, couples face a special ambience so unlike their initial perceptions of *love*. The new atmosphere is shaped according to the peculiar personal needs and personalities of partners, which is hardly ever ethical or logical. Thus, in light of all these clues, both a more sensible view of love and a finer perspective of relationships are useful for resolving some of our misperceptions. The question is why cannot our culture concentrate on factors that are effective in prolonging relationships without relying on love too much, even and especially for starting them? The question is why we cannot identify and depend on relevant factors of relationships' success. The answer is that we really do not appreciate the true nature of love and relationships, nowadays. And we have not yet realized the importance of developing a relationship framework.

Many of us might realize eventually that our perceptions of love and ideal relationships are unrealistic, and thus lower our expectations. We may end up thinking *practical* at the end, but not before hurting our partners and ourselves a long time by letting our idealism and misperceptions raise our expectations naively. The meaning of 'practical' in this instance refers to a form of submission (resignation and disappointment), which usually prevails in relationships these days. Often we learn our lessons too late, instead of thinking practical from the start in the sense of merely perceiving and working on success factors in relationships. Thus, most modern marriages suffer big doses of resignation and disappointment. On the other hand, many good companionship opportunities are lost due to our childish demands. We ruin our marriages or look for an idol until most of our useful lives are wasted on dreams. Some of us might then further damage our integrity, pride, and beliefs when we keep lowering our expectations drastically for getting into a relationship to elude loneliness, despite its obvious flaws and predictable headaches.

Happiness

Happiness is a myth all by itself, but expecting relationships to provide it is too idealistic. We have difficulty even defining it, as it is not a stable state or experience. Yet, we like to perceive it as a lasting state of joy and tranquility, which we also expect to result from our endless materialistic desires, competitions, greed, and shoddy relationships. This is a big conflict already. We want happiness to fit our crooked, materialistic lifestyles, rather than a lifestyle that can stir peace of mind as the closest state of happiness. Instead, happiness needs a big change of mindset and lifestyle (mainly towards selflessness), which only a few of us might eventually find the courage to adopt.

Besides, humans' crude nature does not support happiness and tranquility due to their innate urges for challenge, power, controversy, domination, competition, greed, survival, etc. Anger, hatred, jealousy, spite, and aggression feel so natural, but we should try hard to be honest, compassionate, genuine, and all the other good stuff. Life is not a happy journey, either. Our occasional taste of happiness and tranquility soon faces new dilemmas and disappointments. Thus, as a main step for finding tranquility and improving our relationships, we should actually learn that happiness is a myth and not a stable state.

In relationships, the idea of happiness becomes especially too idealistic, since partners expect their relationship and each other to fulfil their illusory perceptions of happiness, including their egotistical and materialistic needs, pleasure, sexuality, and everlasting tranquility. This expectation is actually one major cause of relationship breakdowns and personal pains. Partners deprive themselves from the basic privileges of relationships, because they believe relationships are meant to bring them happiness. They cause themselves and each other pain with their obsession for happiness through relationships. We have imposed this ironic condition on ourselves in recent decades. Instead of learning the art of selflessness and contentment, partners try to strengthen their identities in relationships and society through arrogance, and then expect happiness, too.

Furthermore, we mistake pleasures (especially sexuality) with happiness, or assume that more pleasures stir happiness. Thus, most relationships become instable soon enough, only because they fail to satisfy our fantastic appetite for happiness and sexuality. Of course, we cannot avoid the impression that companionship can fulfil many of our personal needs. Still, depending on others or relationships to satisfy our personal needs and bring us happiness is naïve and the leading cause of our sufferings. For getting even a chance to taste this elusive happiness, we must seek it within ourselves according to our mental capacity and awareness.

Happiness is a complex topic for discussion, especially within the context of our crooked social values. Many books are written about this topic and maybe another one is due to explain the connection between happiness and relationships in more details. A big collection of happiness definitions can be found in *On Happiness*, by Nima Omidi, Perennial Books, 2014. This author's book, *the Mysteries of Life, Love, and Happiness*, is also a good source.

The natural conclusion in most 'happiness' books is that it may be found only inside a person and he/she needs a special mindset to understand and effect this state. This is what this book advocates as well with an emphasis on becoming better humans through personal awareness, to contact our spirits and become needless about many artificial facets of life in the new era. However, this book also emphasizes on staying practical and understanding our humanistic limitations, which hinder our efforts to be content and a better person.

Some books (quoting philosophers, Buddhism, and the Dalai Lama) suggest that life's purpose is to find happiness. Some of us have reservations about this notion, because we believe life does not have a purpose by itself and humans have many other ambitions besides happiness. The purpose of life (in the context of creation) is neither to spread happiness nor to create good human beings. Happiness is not even the main purpose of one's life per se (regardless of the purpose of the universe). Life is merely a collection of events and moments that transpires in people's lives according to natural laws and chances and affects them based on their cognition (i.e., beliefs, awareness, intelligence, etc.). We all prefer happiness because suffering hurts, and not because it is the purpose of life. We have many higher ambitions in life that we often pursue with greater zeal than our desire for happiness or even pleasures, e.g., need for love, power, or recognition. Most of us simply cannot sit idle and be happy with our contentment. We resent boredom and we crave more adventures even if they cause pain. We want to be loved, although it leads to disappointment and suffering often. The point is that we are not born to be happy or good humans and these are not the purposes of life. We want to become better human beings to soothe our hurts, release tension, or because we sometimes prefer (or like to pretend) to be at peace with ourselves and our surroundings. Happiness and goodness are the probable outcomes of our personal choices to establish the right balance between our ambitions and contentment. Overall, life does not have any particular meaning, nor is it about anything in particular. Just in case life is about something or has a meaning, God has not yet revealed it to us through His prophets, nor has He given us enough intelligence to figure it out ourselves.

The slogan 'life is for the purpose of happiness' is in fact causing more suffering than guiding people towards happiness. The reason is that it makes people believe that such a myth (happiness) actually exists, and that the reason they cannot find it is due to their stupidity or relationships. Thus, they feel edgy, incompetent, and frustrated. They leave their not-so-bad relationships prematurely or seek all kinds of vile pleasures and sexuality to attain the purpose of life, i.e., happiness. But then they feel even more empty and lost.

Most importantly, life is not for the purpose of getting hung up over a mythical concept like happiness and causing extra suffering for ourselves. Ninety-nine percent of us cannot find that elusive happiness. The tiny group who claims to have found it, like monks and priests, should make many sacrifices, limit their social activities, and accept celibacy and suffering in order to maintain their state of contentment, which they call happiness. Happiness appears to demand a lot selflessness, meditation, celibacy, solitude, and sacred sufferings. However, by nature, most of us are selfish, and cherish our sexuality and pleasures a lot, which would accordingly lead to unhappiness. How many of us are willing to be celibate, limit our pleasures and social lives, and welcome sufferings to reach the height of enlightenment (for happiness)? We must really force ourselves to fulfil most of these requirements, which indicates happiness can never be a natural pursuit of humans, particularly in our materialistic world. Accordingly, the purpose of our existence is not to seek happiness, as the Dalai Lama says, because we humans are not prepared to pay the price for it and we are not made for it. Maybe he is referring to 'contentment,' which is different from happiness. Seeking happiness might be a wrong strategy for many of us, indeed, as it appears to be against our nature. Instead, we must mature as a being naturally first. We must think and act within our natural capacities, while aiming to be better human, too. Thus, blaming our relationships and partners for not stirring the happiness that we cannot find on our own is a silly attitude prevalent in society, nowadays.

Ironically, the fact that we crave happiness in vain reveals our deep inner turmoil and inability to define our existence in simpler terms personally.

Trust

The level of mistrust in society and relationships is rising too fast due to humans' tricky hormones, people's bad experiences, and corruptive social environment in the new era. Obviously, the success of any relationship depends on the goodness of its partners. However, individuals' characteristics, behaviour, and nature reveal the inherent shortfalls of humans, especially for socializing. Actually, it might be easier to prove that humans become more arrogant and unreliable the more they socialize and as time goes by. Thus, it becomes harder for them to relate and trust one another in relationships and communities. All the facts show that the chances of creating even a small society of pure humans are slim, because they would not be allowed to choose their lifestyles against social norms. Developing pure humans within the crooked value systems of modern society simply feels like a funny concept. It sounds like a mission to nurture edible fish in a polluted swamp. With the speed we are destroying the environment, where nature is meant to flourish itself and embrace us too, how could a puritan emerge?

These conclusions are again depressing in terms of human trustworthiness. They also confirm humans' vast limitations to grasp the requirements of relationships and coping with them. Then again, if we admit that human nature is impure, we might learn to keep our expectations from relationships and people low. We get less surprised and frustrated about their duplicity, while we grow some form of understanding and compassion towards our partners and helpless humanity.

Obviously, we benefit psychologically to assume that we can try to become better beings than we have been so far. We know that we have spiritual tendencies and can improve our awareness level and tranquility with meditation. But are we made to be a peaceful and logical species? Do we understand 'logic'? Does our logic have any meaning or significance? It is hard to judge. However, I doubt it personally. We have not yet been able to demonstrate such capacity. Yet, since human is not inherently pure and trustworthy, maybe we must try even harder, against our nature, to become a bit purer and better in order to serve ourselves in such a harsh social environment.

Nevertheless, we might adjust our level of marital mistrust in a progressive manner by considering the following points:

1. Our accurate perceptions of social corruption and duplicity cause cynicism about people's truthfulness and authenticity. This personal wisdom and warranted defence mechanism might inadvertently stir a large level of misperceptions and mistrusts in relationships. Many misperceptions are also due to our own idiosyncrasies or communication hurdles.
2. The high ratio and repercussions of marital failures simply make relationships too risky in the new era. Thus, absolute caution about the words and promises of our partners seems quite warranted.
3. Mistrust is a natural (and usually necessary) condition in relationships in the new era. This is a logical consequence of social life and not an indication of a person's weakness or selfishness. However, partners' mistrust is also often caused by their own oversensitivity and misperceptions, which then affects their attitude and added mistrust. In general, partners must remain conscious of the high possibility of, and many causes for, misjudging each other.
4. We must stop expecting our partners to trust us completely, especially when deep down we feel the difficulty of doing the same thing ourselves.
5. We can never know *who we are* or *who they are* and they can never know *who they are* or *who we are*. We should honour these two facts open-mindedly. We struggle all our lives to find ourselves and happiness, to no avail. So how can we expect others to know us and trust us when even we do not? It is simply impossible to build complete trust based on our doubtful perceptions of ourselves and others.

6. We should not consider love and trust as main factors of relationships' health anymore. They are deceptive, illogical yardsticks. People often lie about their love or trust to avoid confrontations, or just for being tactful and wise. Expecting trust or love beyond people's natural capacity would only bring more duplicity and phoniness into relationships.
7. We should come to terms with two major facts in the new era: a) it is natural for couples to lose trust in each other somewhat, and b) we must learn to live in relationships with imperfect trust levels, instead of making a big issue about it. We should be ultra cautious when starting our relationships, but then remain flexible about inevitable disappointments and mistrust later on.

The fact that we should try so hard to become better human beings and find happiness shows that humans are not pure by nature and they are not trustworthy. However, acknowledging our impurity should motivate us to overcome our Egos and try harder to understand the meaning and process of becoming a better human; not merely because it would be a social ideal, but because it would make us happier at the end. The simple fact that Ego is an inherent part of the human psyche is enough to stir their bias, selfishness, hypocrisy, and many other flaws. The fact that we are so greedy and competitive, and the way we love capitalism, materialism, and pleasures show that we are impure by nature. The mere fact that Christians believe Jesus died because of their sins—and similar beliefs in other religions—shows humans' tendency to sin. The fact that so many relationships fail nowadays, and the way partners treat each other at the time of separation, show their impurity; it also shows people's inability to get along, trust one another, and show compassion. The fact that we must constantly go for confessions and repentance, to cleanse our souls, is another clue about our impurity. Humans' historical and rising needs for more prisons, wars, and stronger judicial systems reveal the deep impurity of humans as well as the societies they have been able to build after millenniums of philosophizing and experimenting.

The fact that we do good things and charity (usually for self-serving purposes, pretences, or to cleanse our conscience) does not wash all other negative tendencies in human nature. Purity is not a matter of comparing the number of good deeds versus bad ones, either, even if people did more good than bad. Purity is just an absolute fact and not an algebraic equation. It either exists or not. Even doing one bad thing indicates the impurity of human nature. And we must be blind not to see it at such a high dosage. The only question is how often humans' impurity turns into evil. Too often and globally, it feels! Then, with so much impurity around us, keeping our trust in others, even our family members, has become a very tough job.

Commitment

The above points about mistrust in relationships and human nature in general show that relying on our partners, or their promises, would be rather naïve. Accordingly, expecting them to fulfil their commitments, especially in terms of staying in their relationships, does not sound like a wise strategy. Yet, deep down, we all imagine that relationships' longevity is still a valid expectation in the new era. Thanks to our traditional mentality, a big misperception in society and people's minds is that relationships must last forever. These days, however, this is the least likely scenario considering the statistics on divorce, family problems, strive for individualism, sexuality, and the growing level of stress in society. So now, it is time to view relationships more in terms of an open-ended arrangement, instead of a lasting commitment. In the author's opinion, we must indeed look forward with great excitement for this rather radical mindset to propagate. The reason is that the advantages of this kind of relationship arrangement—with a set expiry date perhaps—might amaze us in the end. This would prove to be one of those rare instances where reverse psychology works very well. That is, the couples' knowledge of their relationship's high vulnerability would goad them to stay vigilant about its health. They simply try hard to protect their relationship in a positive, teamwork environment. They realize that they should work on their relationship with care regularly to keep it, rather than taking it for granted and letting it expire at a preset date. Actually, if partners (or some legal mechanism) set a definite timeframe along with an *automatic expiry of their marriage obligation at* a fixed point, couples would stay together much longer than they would have under the present circumstance, as they get serious in finding good reasons for renewing and prolonging their relationship. This reverse psychology would definitely help our societies in at least five ways, too:

- Couples get into their relationships more carefully based on intelligent analyses of their needs, compatibility, and the suitability of a particular relationship model for them.
- Couples work harder and more consciously to prolong their relationships instead of letting it expire. This would most likely increase the longevity of most relationships that are worth saving.
- Couples are mentally prepared to leave their relationships with the least amount of shock and hassle when a particular relationship is not working. They know from the beginning that, when necessary, separation is a good and acceptable possibility.
- Ending relationships is automatic and hassle free.
- Most of all, partners' idiotic, useless desire for commitment and its reliability will become obsolete.

The point is that we need modern thinking and principles for relationships to match the modern life we are so eagerly embracing. Along with our modern lifestyles and thirst for individualism, we would also behave more in line with the humans' innate sexual tendencies and hormones noted below.

We are addressing our sexuality more liberally every day with lesser concern about social ethics, anyway. Therefore, viewing relationships as a temporary arrangement might be the only logical solution for the dilemma of relationships, considering the rising rate of relationship failures, our sizzling sexuality, and our eagerness to have a companion, too, anyway. If we learn to perceive our relationships *merely* as a conditional companionship, which might entail a family, too, then we can possibly define a set of relationship principles appropriate for the modern life and then set our expectations accordingly.

Some people have already reached similar conclusions, thus building their relationships more freely. They do not fuss over marriage formalities, such as a license or religious ritual. In another type of relationships, mostly common in developing societies (where romantic fantasies have not still corrupted partners' cultural view of relationships) couples rely largely on tradition or religious principles to maintain their relationships. However, the rest of us believe that neither of these kinds of relationships is appropriate. We disapprove these approaches since partners are not bound by official documents or they are not marrying based on love. We perceive these relationships valueless, because in our modern thinking we have learned to see relationships as a love-union. Yet, at the same time, we insist on legal documents and court system to protect us when love erodes. We all know that our naive love has a good chance of faltering sooner or later. Yet, we insist on ignoring this information at the outset. It is a big irony that we wish to base our marriages on love and trust, but in fact do not trust each other's promise to live together merely on the strength of the presumed love. We demand a marriage license and legal protection. Love without trust! This is surely hypocritical, but also an obvious contradiction. It shows our hunch about the high risks of both love and relationships, nowadays. We insist on legal protection for the chance of the marriage breakdown, but we are too shy and romantic to sign a contract that dictates partners' rights upon their marriage breakdown without any need to go to court. We should now insist on implementing this progressive and practical practice.

Equality

Nowadays, we try to oversimplify, or perhaps even abuse, the purposes of relationship principles by pushing the concept of equality and assuming it would solve all our social and marital problems automatically. We have attempted in the new era to remedy women's personal problems thru equality and reduce the amount of intimidation and control by men. Yet, we have not solved the problems of relationships. Actually, relationship conflicts have raised dramatically in society as the concept of equality has been stressed. Even worse, women's frustration has risen due to their unfulfilled expectations. Their growing expectations from relationships have merely caused them more agony and deprivation (again judging by divorce rates and growing family conflicts).

Often, women's expectations for equality seem bizarre and vague, sounding like whining, with devastating effect on their relationships. Some women's exaggerated demand for equality sometimes sounds more like a quest for superiority. Initially, the equality movement appeared logical for subduing men's domination. But now, everything seems to be turning around. That is, men feel unequal in a world where women set most standards of equality, which seem one-sided or arbitrary. They often feel intimidated by their wives' wild wishes and vague expectations. Many men have adopted a passive role in their relationships due to the severity of their spouses' views of equality. The problem is that, nowadays, 'equality bargaining' is infected by partners' Ego.

Equality expectations often arise from partners' urge to control one another. The notion of equality is psychologically absurd, anyway. This is because everyone inherently believes that his/her logic is superior to other people's, including his/her criteria for defining equality. We strongly believe that we know about everything better than everybody else regardless of their genders. A strong tendency exists in most humans to feel superior to others, not equal, although they might pretend to be fair and humble. In modern societies, almost everybody believes in gender equality, but not intellectual equality. By default, our Ego forces us to feel almost perfect in terms of logic, intelligence, cognition and all the rest of the good stuff. The gender equality issue is resolved largely, but the inherent sense of superiority can never be erased from people's minds —due to their wild perception of their intellectual superiority. This is the source of all the inequalities, nowadays. They are not gender driven, but rather Ego directed for both genders. Gender equality is a hot issue, now, due to the relationships' rising importance and troubles in society, and since everybody (men and women) feels special and superior and not equal.

Equality is, by the way, perceived and measured differently by people according to their subjective criteria and emotional maturity. Thus, instead of wasting so much energy on forcing some kind of imaginary equality in relationships, couples must learn to put all those efforts into defining a practical process of teamwork. Teamwork enables couples to contribute to major decisions and feel active in their relationships. Yet, it does not deprive partners from doing most tasks independently based on their expertise or just for creating synergy. Partners must be able to decide independently, instead of always doubting their authority or identity due to some fake rules of equality. They must not lose their confidence and control of their lives in fear of retaliation.

The concept of 'equality' has initially emerged out of a sense of desperation among women, but is now being driven mostly by Ego—the urge for superiority. Teamwork, on the other hand, is Self (goodness) and Model (tactfulness) driven. Thus, it is not too hard to decide which approach could have a better chance of success in the long run. Couples' quarrels to stir equality would only reinforce the Egos of both partners, and thus more clashes. Besides, as said before, the concept of equality is psychologically flawed, anyway, since our fervent Ego abhors equality. People are psychologically incapable of handling equality, as they feel superior in their deepest level of consciousness.

While equality, in the sense of *fairness,* is the foundation of our democratic society, it has turned into a socio-political platform to further spread our demented social values. The term 'equality' is somewhat misused inadvertently to express our repressed anxieties and insecurities, which then leads to the creation of formidable expectations and headaches. Sadly, the meaning and implication of equality are exaggerated, so much so it has ruined the structure of relationships altogether.

Human Hormones' Role

Mostly social chaos in modern societies can be blamed for people's vast misperceptions and attitude regarding happiness, equality, love, trust, and commitment, which then lead to both relationship conundrums and further social chaos. However, human hormones are now playing a more active role regarding the growing relationship problems in the new era, because so little ethical and moral principles exist these days to curb the effects of instinctual and hormonal attributes of humans.

Without getting into too much technical discussions about human hormones, the following scientific findings show the author's overall grasp of hormones' effect on our behaviours and relationships:

- While sexual activity triggers our mood for cuddling and attachment, too much sex most likely erodes the sense of attachment in the long run.
- Although attachment might increase sexual urge initially, prolonged attachment often dampens the urge for sex.

- Romance and attachment are not proven to be related.
- Attachment might erode romance.
- Romance might subdue sexual urges.
- Humans are not built to be monogamous, contrary to some animals that have the right chemistry for it.
- The hot sense of passion often dies within six months to about two years.
- Humans' chemistry (and instincts) draws them to different people for fulfilling their romantic, attachment, and sexual urges.
- The effects of human hormones on people and their mood swings, especially for women during childbirth, menstrual cycle, and menopause, contribute to the growing gender differences and relationship clashes.

Relationships' Role and Capacity

Our growing expectations in all fronts, especially about love, happiness, trust, commitment, and equality (as reviewed in this chapter) are stirring lots of conflicts and marital breakdowns. Couples' formidable expectations are responsible for the fast demise of relationships environment in the new era. Again, the problem is that we have misunderstood the role and capacity of relationships to satisfy so many of our wild expectations that have been briefly discussed in this chapter.

We have arbitrarily mixed traditional family values with so many new personal ideals and created huge misperceptions in our minds about the purposes and capacity of relationships. This condition surely cannot prevail if we intend to improve relationships' health. Yet we like our progressive lifestyles and mentalities so much, nowadays. Therefore, the only solution is to at least adjust our mentalities about the role and capacity of relationships, reduce our vast and confusing expectations, and find means of coping with the new reality. Every couple must also choose a relationship model suitable for their personalities in terms of the amount of independence and individualism they seek so keenly these days. For making even this basic adjustment in our mentalities about the reality of relationships, people must recognize common misperceptions in society that cause deep miscommunications and frictions in relationships. In particular, they should grasp the effects of their delusions about trust, commitment, equality, love, happiness, and the role of human hormones.

The above facts demonstrate our idealism about humans' ability to honour their marriage commitments, love, monogamy, and to maintain some reasonable amount of trust in their relationships. Many radical conclusions can be drawn in line with these natural human tendencies: On the one hand, the effects of hormones on our behaviour somewhat suggest that we should not really feel too guilty for being so sexually inclined and losing our willpower to honour our wedding vows and relationship commitments. They also suggest that we should not get too mad and frustrated with our cheating spouses, either, if we could logically see their helplessness about all these tricks of Nature. On the other hand, we cannot stop wondering about humans' ability to be a bit more ethical and have some level of integrity and self-control, despite all their natural tendencies. What kind of society and relationship atmosphere we humans really need and can support?

Overall, in line with topics discussed above, we can make the following observations about relationships' reality in modern societies[‡]:

1. Relationships get into trouble often because partners are not conscious of its needs and goals or when they find them in major conflicts with their personal goals.

---

‡ Nearly 1,000 facts and trends in this author's book, *Relationship Facts, Trends, and Choices* provide further proof about the current sad reality of relationships.

2. Couples must learn to view relationships as an independent entity with specific needs and objectives of its own, which are different from partners' personal objectives and needs. These needs must get precedence over personal needs.
3. Boundaries should be set between partners' personal needs (or goals) and the relationship needs in order to minimize conflicts.
4. A practical framework must be developed to define the needs, objectives, and boundaries of relationships.
5. This relationship framework must also define the factors and characteristics of a successful relationship.
6. The major role of a relationship framework is to enforce teamwork while increasing the effectiveness of partners' communication.
7. As personal needs change in society gradually over a few decades, the relationship framework must also be adjusted accordingly in order to reduce frictions.
8. Partners' need for independence and individuality should be given the highest priority in developing this relationship framework.
9. The main tool to achieve to align personal and relationship needs is to reduce couples' expectations from relationships.
10. Like any kind of machinery or system, relationships also require routine checks and balances to remain functional.
11. Partners' biggest challenge is to find the right relationship model for their mixed personalities and to function within its parameters. They must stop guessing what a relationship is or what they like it to be.
12. The onus is placed on partners to stay objective and fair by respecting their relationship needs and boundaries in order to prolong their marriage.

Chapter Three

Relationships Success Factors

A relationship prospers when partners grasp and observe its needs, while respecting each other. It thrives even better when both partners are *good* and *enlightened*. 'Good' means partners' knack to rely more on their conscience and Self than Ego for relating to each other naturally. 'Enlightened' means partners realize humans' inherent limitations and have low expectations from relationships. They realize their own idiosyncrasies and sympathize with their partners' struggle with similar inner and outer forces beyond their control.

Clearly, these tough conditions restrict the opportunity for building good relationships vastly, considering the difficulty of being good and enlightened individuals, nowadays. The chance of both partners being good and enlightened is even less. Just the opposite: Genetic defects, sexuality, and crooked lifestyles make most of us rigid with huge Egos. We are crippled by our misperceptions about life purposes and who we are. Thus, we seldom give ourselves a chance to learn about some of the finer means of thinking and living. Even when we do, we have big difficulties staying on a self-awareness path when people around us are consumed with superficial needs and spread phony values. For example, it is difficult to resist the niceties of 'consumerism' when the whole world is embracing it so dearly. It is hard to overcome one's obsession for 'equality' and show patience for teamwork. How could one not follow those seemingly progressive and rational social ideologies? How could one explain one's passivity and modesty to one's obsessed companion or friends? Our needs for conformity and Egos would not allow us to mature mentally and resist luring temptations and superficiality. These examples are not meant to refute the need for 'equality' or to criticize consumerism. Rather, they reflect that social trends usually override even our purest personal beliefs, logic, or good intentions.

Therefore, we should now view relationships in a new light and fathom solutions that fit the emerging, irreversible course of history. We should identify realistic success factors to guide us and empower our relationships, despite the growing sources of their dysfunctionality. The success factors must correspond with our modern social structure and our increasing demand for independence and individuality. Instead of looking for an ideal, imaginary companion and relationship environment, our new goal must be to make relationships only manageable and tolerable. It is time to lower our expectations by developing a workable framework. This sounds like an ambitious goal, but if we are lucky and lucid we might be able to create a modern relationship framework mostly by (and for) balancing couples' personal needs with relationship's unique needs.

No one knows the parameters of a successful relationship due to rapid social changes that have tainted most people's perceptions, personalities, and relationships. Thus, we usually list out some relationship objectives, such as love, security, longevity, and wealth, as indicators of relationships' success. We also consider 'communication' a crucial factor for the success of relationships. Those who have suffered the negative experiences of relationships are cynical about the possibility of building successful relationships, anyway. To this pessimistic group, relationships can be nothing but hell.

With no understanding of relationship needs and success factors, nowadays, we create our own subjective perceptions about the purposes and potentials of relationships based on our personal needs and a large variety of superficial values pushed on us in our rampant societies. We develop a fantasy in our heads regarding the purposes of relationships and their success factors. Accordingly, we set ourselves up for disappointment, since our naïve expectations cannot be fulfilled.

Our prevalent misperceptions regarding relationships were discussed in the previous chapter. The bottomline is that we (as a society) no longer have a realistic grasp of relationships and its purposes, let alone the knowledge of factors making them successful. Our deformed educational systems, especially at senior high school, have failed to teach this vital real life subject to the group of people who need this knowledge so urgently. It is a pity that such an important matter, with such grave effect on social wellbeing, is left to the public's personal perceptions and interpretations, instead of being researched for society's benefit and taught at high school to everybody. Sadly, people and governments have lost track of human priorities. Hopefully, we soon realize the gloomy prospect of humanity without a fundamental social awakening.

Nevertheless, to study relationships, we should build, 1) a definition for it, 2) a list of success factors for it, and 3) a list of partners' realistic expectations from it.

A Definition of Relationships

A relationship is mainly a collection of activities and feelings shared by partners. Yet, it must also be viewed as a functional setting for goading partners' teamwork to achieve certain goals. These purposes are of two kinds: First, the goals that fulfil the realistic personal and joint needs of partners. Second, the goals aimed at maintaining the health of the relationship itself. We usually do not realize or ignore the latter.

Thus, a comprehensive definition for relationships is:

> A *relationship is a functional setting with specific needs and goals to sustain itself, which only then might fulfil partners' realistic goals, too.*

This definition emphasizes on relationship needs and goals before a relationship can be of any use to couples. Clearly, couples must show willingness and patience to learn and fulfil these relationships' special needs to strengthen their marriages. They should view 'relationships' as an independent entity with unique, inherent needs. Surely, the process of recognizing and using this unorthodox relationship principle would be gradual, because couples should learn to reduce their expectations from relationships and attend to their personal needs independently more often. Therefore, the first thing to study is the viability of people's expectations from modern relationships.

Modern Relationship Expectations

To develop a realistic list of relationship expectations for the new era, we can outline couples' ideal, common expectations, as shown in Table 3.1 on the next page. Then, we can review and eliminate those that are conflicting with partners' personal needs, in particular for independence and individuality. After all, relationships' toughest challenge these days is to develop a peaceful environment and accommodate both partners' craving for so many complex, clashing needs with minimal frictions.

An ideal relationship would satisfy all the expectations in Table 3.1 and more. However, we must aim only for the ones that can fit the majority of relationships based on our modern mentalities and lifestyles. Discussions in the following pages will show why many of these expectations are hard to achieve, nowadays; thus the need to exclude them in order to reduce the useless pressure on relationships and to minimize partners' disappointments. This would be contrary to what couples are doing nowadays, as they assume relationship expectations can be a natural extension of their increasing personal needs.

Table 3.1: A Preliminary List of General Expectations from Relationships

1. Sex
2. Financial Security
3. Communication
4. Companionship – Relate
5. Teamwork
6. Love: SLove, ELove, MLove
7. Trust
8. Happiness – Peace of mind, tranquility, joy
9. Friendship – Loyalty, honesty, etc.
10. Respect- Social acceptance
11. Personal Success
12. Commitment
13. Longevity
14. Financial Stability
15. Compassion
16. Dependence- support

As society promotes phonier lifestyles, the complexity and level of partners' expectations have kept growing. Everybody believes s/he deserves to live like movie stars. Yet, the reality is just the opposite. That is, partners' level of expectations from relationships should be reduced largely to compensate for the rising pressures that society is placing on the personal lives of people already. They have enough distress outside the house already without the need for more pressures from their relationships, too. Then, they must also refine their mentalities and reduce their expectations in line with their rising emphasis on personal identity, independence, and individualism. In fact, in some special cases, all the expectations in Table 3.1 may be fulfilled in a relationship. Yet, as a rule, we must satisfy most of these personal needs independently. Now let us review the expectations listed in Table 3.1 and pinpoint the unrealistic ones.

1. Sex: This is the most natural expectation from relationships. Since couples *attempt* not to look outside their marriages to fulfil this basic need, they must rely on their relationships for it. Yet, in reality, spouses, often withdraw sex (rather naturally) as a tool for emotional blackmail or retaliation. Moreover, partners cannot cooperate in this regard sometimes, thus seek sex elsewhere. Nonetheless, nothing can be done regarding this need beyond what everybody knows and practices already the best way they can or feel. This is a legitimate expectation from relationships. All the dramas surrounding sex cannot be helped either. Most of them are psychologically explainable and rather inevitable. The only advice is to grasp the role of sex more realistically and compassionately, instead of using it for blackmailing and hurting our partners.

2. Financial Security is a rather obsolete concept, although many relationships still rely on one member of the family to be the main breadwinner. The point is that financial security is no longer an automatic arrangement like the old times. People do (should) not get into relationships for financial security any more when society revolves around 'independence.' Financial security in relationships, when it occurs, is mainly by accident or some kind of agreement between partners. It is merely an exception, not an expectation. Financial security is no longer a norm, but a possible by-product of being in a relationship and only in the spirit of teamwork.

In all, partners (must) get into relationships, nowadays, with confidence in their abilities to support themselves financially if their relationships do not work out. It seems silly these days to envision couples get into relationships for financial security, although many do so stealthily. While financial dependence worked in the past, it feels increasingly incongruent with the popular principle of partners' equality, which is so seriously pursued, particularly by women. Surely, many couples would continue to prefer dependency on their partners. It would be difficult to draw the lines so rigidly (about independence). However, here we are talking about *setting mindsets* that are realistic and congruent with partners' overall perspective about relationships' progressive format in the new era. Relationships would continue to fail due to so many factors. Only one of them would be partners' reluctance to be self-sufficient and competent and just hoping that a relationship would rectify their financial insecurity. Nowadays, partners must somehow understand and agree on the mechanism of their household finance, too, before they commit themselves to a relationship. Accordingly, the more relevant topic that requires scrutiny now is 'financial control' and not 'financial security.'

In terms of financial control, also, the trend is changing. In the recent past, financial control referred to situations where one or both partners insisted on (or fought about) controlling the whole financial affair, even if the other partner made all the money. Even though both partners rather discussed some aspects of financial decisions, usually one partner ended up being more in control of financial issues and bank accounts (although they usually shared the accounts). Now, they must be responsible for their own share of the pie, whether they have earned it themselves or is allotted to them through some type of family budget. Financial autonomy is now an essential factor that partners should discuss and plan at the outset. Thus, the phrase 'Financial Control' is now more properly referring to the fact that each partner should keep financial control over his/her own financial affair. The other partner must not expect otherwise. The matter of sharing income, and possible joint investments, is also a reasonable arrangement when it is done voluntarily through cooperation and teamwork, but never as an expectation anymore. Those of us still in the transition stage must overhaul our mentalities.

Another major issue regarding family finances is partners' knack for 'financial stability' that is discussed below (item 14) separately due to its importance.

3. Communication is the essence of successful relationships and a crucial expectation mainly for enforcing teamwork. Still, many good relationships are ruined by simple misperceptions and miscommunications. Partners' oversensitivity, arrogance, and false pride often hinder even common dialogues. Effective communication is, nowadays, also vital for implementing a hassle-free separation when necessary. Instead of spending time and money on lawyers, a prenuptial contract, plus partners' objectivity, can boost communication during separation when it becomes inevitable. Sadly, however, effective communication is the toughest expectation from relationships, since partners are not trained to communicate properly or their retaliations and Egos obstruct the process.

4. Companionship: This is an automatic expectation meant to reflect partners' wisdom and abilities to relate smoothly in line with a sense of trust and reliance. Yet, we often alienate our partners quickly due to our egoism and misperceptions about marital life. We do not quite know the purposes or means of benefiting from the basic privilege of relationships. Moreover, our initial perceptions regarding our companion usually prove to be erroneous before long, thus we get confused about our marriage, too. Partners' ability to relate is an important topic explained in more detail in Chapter Eight.

We all like to have a companion, and relationships provide this opportunity, but the question is whether we prefer a lousy companion to loneliness. We seek high-quality companions to get compassion and love. A companion should be like this or that, we imagine, while we strive to satisfy our needs for love. However, finding an ideal companion is largely a matter of luck, especially since we have no proper education regarding the purpose and process of companionship. Sadly, not enough wise, humble people exist who grasp the art of companionship and can share it with one another in a peaceful relationship environment. Thus, while companionship remains an inherent and valid expectation, its effectiveness is doomed.

5. Teamwork: Couples' capacity for teamwork is the main success factor in relationships. As we insist on independence and individualism so keenly, the need for teamwork becomes even greater in order to keep our big Egos under a leash. For teamwork, partners must clearly have some inherent qualities, including modesty and objectivity. Yet, people's *obsession for individualism* hinders both their *modesty and objectivity* these days. Therefore, finding companions of such high quality and implementing teamwork in relationships would be a major challenge. Still, teamwork is an absolute necessity and should be considered a basic expectation for successful relationships.

For managing the 'relationship needs' and responding to at least some of our partners' personal needs, we should commit ourselves to teamwork and learn about compromising. The urgency for teamwork is not still appreciated, since couples consider it a threat to their independence and authority. Yet, teamwork is the only tool available to couples to coordinate and monitor the manner of satisfying their relationships' needs. Thus, it should become a major expectation soon, with some training to go along with it. The methods of family teamwork must be developed soon, too.

6. Love: Love *might* make couples' communication smoother and more effective. It *could* also help them satisfy their needs for compassion. However, love does not qualify as a legitimate expectation from relationships, due to its illusive nature. We all like to taste love at least for starting a relationship and love is a good gauge for weighing the degree of partners' attraction and success in satisfying their sexual need. However, we must not consider love a reliable factor to keep partners together. Love is not an objective measure for assessing relationships' success, either. The reason is obvious. When we express love, we are influenced by a perception of Selfless love (SLove), while we are driven mostly by our Ego and love deficiency (ELove). Everybody has this spiritual need, SLove, to love someone or something passionately. When we meet a person who can stir this feeling in us, we consume ourselves with a perception of SLove. This individual becomes a mirage that fulfils our need for SLove. All along, our need for ELove (ego-ridden deficiency love) further encourages us to identify this person as our soul mate. We are suddenly in love. This is great for bringing couples together. Yet, true SLove happens only rarely and only when partners are rather needless and enlightened persons. Thus, our perception of SLove is only a transitory 'perception' and not a reality. ELove, on the other hand, is an absolute reality and not a perception. Thus, ELove keeps putting more demands on partners every day, because its only purpose is to feed partners' selfish need for attention. It creates possessiveness, jealousy, and frustration.

Let us use MLove as a term to signify a sense of civilized, tactful expression of love. It helps people express their natural (unexaggerated) emotions and sweeten their relationships, too. Therefore, MLove could be listed as a valid expectation from relationships, with some reservation. The reservation relates to the nature of MLove, as it is not genuine enough to count on its lasting effectiveness. MLove contains role-playing and it lacks adequate authenticity. Its effect depends on the strength of a person's talent for playing his/her role naturally. Yet, not everybody can be good at it. On the other hand, MLove can help a lot to keep romance alive in relationships.

Many radical ideas proposed in this book make the nature of relationships look too impersonal and cold. This picture of pessimism might prove to be the reality we must eventually face in line with the values and culture we are embracing so fast and enthusiastically, often inadvertently. Thus, MLove is a helpful and relatively realistic expectation to stir passion and compassion in relationships. It *might* also be useful for keeping partners alert and proactive regarding their relationship needs, especially teamwork and communication.

In general, however, love, as we express it so readily these days, is not going to help relationships. Therefore, **we must remove love as a legitimate expectation from relationships** (except for MLove). We can apply 'love' as a yardstick for attraction and for facilitating communication, but not as a valid factor of relationship success.

The overall demand for love in society far exceeds the supply. We all seek love too much, but do not know how to give love. We think we do, but, for reasons noted throughout this book, we are only assuming to know what love is and how we can offer it to others. Again, the supply and demand for love (all three kinds, i.e., SLove, ELove, and MLove) are quite unbalanced and causing undue pressure on people' lives and society in general. We have become too needy for love since everything else in society is stressful. And we assume that by showing love to someone, he/she gains the power or expertise to offer the genuine empathy we need to curb social pressures.

The notations SLove, ELove, and MLove mentioned above have the following definitions in this book:

- SLove (selfless love) is the purest kind of love we feel towards our children, Nature, and possibly for our artistic creations. With SLove, we Serve (give) love Selflessly without expecting to get love in return. Thus, prefix 'S' could also stand for 'Serving.'
- ELove (egotistic love) reflects the selfish need for love and attention and is mostly a reflection of insecurity. With ELove, people demand (Expect) love egotistically. Thus, 'E' could also stand for 'Expecting.'
- MLove (model love) is the tactful expressions of love to show compassion and cope with social etiquette. With MLove, we try to Moderate our relationships Modestly with our tactful Model. Thus, 'M' could also stand for 'Moderating and Modesty.'

7. Trust: Discussions in Chapter Two showed why mistrust is becoming a general condition in relationships, nowadays. Yet, partners must stop fussing about it, and instead live with some degree of mistrust as long as the integrity of their relationship is not jeopardized. Total trust cannot be a valid expectation.

8. Happiness: Chapter Two's points about happiness reveal why it cannot be a valid expectation from relationships, either. We expect our relationships and partners bring us happiness. We expect joy and tranquility as an automatic result of finding a companion. Yet, neither our relationships nor our partners are capable of providing happiness if we are not personally equipped for mastering happiness alone first. Our chance of finding happiness in relationships depends on many factors, but mainly our mental capacity to interpret, absorb, and reflect happiness. In all, happiness is merely a subjective perception, rather than a tangible commodity to expect from relationships. If anything, relationships' environment is too demanding and complex these days to exert happiness. It is our responsibility and art to enjoy our companion, while exploring the merits of being in a relationship. Usually, if we are a happy person, we know how to stir happiness within or without a relationship. The opposite is even truer. If we have no capacity for being happy, relationships normally make us unhappier. Therefore, expecting happiness from our relationships or partners is not realistic. Couples must accept that the only perceivable source of happiness in marriage is the mere presence of a companion in their lives. If partners' presence alone does not stir happiness automatically, their relationship becomes even less credible to induce happiness. Under this circumstance, the couple must either learn to relate (at least passively) or opt for separation, but never keep nagging and demanding love and happiness. Accordingly, the couple must either learn to relate (passively at least) or opt for separation, instead of demanding happiness and love or just keep nagging.

Another irony is that we usually think that relationships can bring us happiness because it can solve our personal problems. This is another false assumption and unrealistic expectation. In fact, this mentality is destroying relationships and reducing its capacity to induce even a slight measure of peace and comfort. As a whole, expecting relationships to solve our problems is a damned expectation. A good relationship helps us mentally to deal with our personal problems more effectively, if we were smart and humble. A bad one, on the other hand, destroys our ability to think straight and take care of even our basic needs, let alone the complicated problems of life and relationships. The statistics show that more relationships fail than succeed. Thus, instead of expecting relationships to solve our problems, we should expect and be ready to face relationship hardships and the high likelihood of separation. We must be prepared for relationships' new headaches, instead of solving our existing problems. That is the goal of this and the other books in this series, too—to prepare the readers for relationship headaches. At the same time, this high awareness may help smart partners perceive the purposes and potentials of relationships in a proper light and thus prevent its demise.

Playing many roles and games to exert happiness would not work, either. Although many experts advocate role-paying to make couples release their tensions and express the sources of their anxiety, this author believes that couples can decide about the viability of their relationships only by understanding the deep-rooted causes of relationship obstacles in the new era. Relying on partners' intelligence to learn the sad truth about relationships works better than keeping them hopeful merely by playing some artificial roles. This is especially true when partners are already under pressure mentally and physically. Role-playing causes more stress and frustration when partners feel the futility of their efforts deep down. Why they feel this way? From experience, we know that once the process of alienation between partners begins, it is almost impossible to return it to its initial state of moderate tranquility around some intelligent principles for partners' coexistence. The only thing that can save relationships is learning the truth about the real causes of problems, which usually relate to partners' own vast, irreparable idiosyncrasies.

9. Friendship: An excellent test of 'relationship success' is partners' ability to enhance their friendship. Yet, this idea has never been promoted as an expectation. Often couples, in fact, prove their inabilities to be close friends, but insist to marry and build a family. The big feature of successful friendships, which is badly missing in relationships, is that friends' limited expectations are set gradually and naturally without pressure or demand. Then, even if those expectations are not fulfilled, they seldom argue or fight over them. They only moderate (realign) their own expectations to keep their friendship. They cherish their friendship so much they curb their expectations willingly. This is actually the strength of good friendships and a main reason for their success and longevity. This is a great tactic to grasp and apply in relationships actively as well. Yet, an exactly opposite mentality prevails in relationships, where couples set high demands immediately, instead of appreciating the value of what they already have, like the way friends do. In fact, couples keep increasing their expectations, rivalries, and whining, until their relationship falls apart. Thus, 'partners' aptitude for friendship' is a vital new expectation that should be analysed and promoted more proactively in relationships. Relationships should be based more on friendship than love.

Friendship is discussed here separately as a success factor (expectation) for modern relationships, although it is actually the highest attribute of companionship (item 4 listed above).

10. Respect/Social Acceptance: While pushing for equality, independence, and identity, modern couples now demand total respect from their partners. This is a sensible expectation that fits social trends. Yet, partners must not merely expect respect. Rather, they should learn to respect their partners despite their clear idiosyncrasies and personality weaknesses.

Society gives a higher status to family than individuals, but we also value our relationships for helping us fit better within the society as useful and respectful individuals. Accordingly, 'respect' is now an automatic rather newer expectation from relationships among all other reasons for getting married.

11. Personal Success: A relationship must facilitate partners' success and growth. This seemingly selfish expectation (need) has a positive consequence for building relationships, though. That is, while stressing on personal success, partners would insist even more on finding the proper relationship model that can best satisfy their personal needs. Otherwise, they should not bother get married. After all, if partners feel successful and fulfilled individually, their marriage would also find a better chance for success. And vice versa. It makes a lot of sense.

Partners' cooperation would give them a higher chance for success in social and personal endeavours, since maximizing synergy and moral support are companionship's main benefits. Accordingly, personal success is a reasonable, useful criterion to include in the list of realistic relationship expectations. In reality, however, the sense of individualism and independence forces partners to compete with each other. Their unrelenting urges for recognition and showing off their independence and identity make them too arrogant at the cost of losing sight of their relationships' basic merits. It is just embarrassing how partners strive to sabotage and hurt each other and ruin their relationships, instead of leaning about the means and benefits of helping and encouraging each other for personal success. Nonetheless, couples must choose the right relationship model according to their personalities and need for achievement, then keep their Egos under a leash as well.

12. Commitment: Relationships have traditionally entailed some form of commitment for partners to stick together even when some aspects of their relationship were not ideal. Maybe 'commitment' was a useful mechanism in the past and even now. Yet, as a practical step, partners should begin to realize that, nowadays, the sense of commitment is vastly eroded by the need for individualism. Now, couples insist on enjoying their lives at the highest level possible. They get out of their relationships fast, sometimes even based on childish reasons or their perceptions of a better life with a different partner. The bottomline is that commitment can no longer be considered a sensible expectation from relationships in the new era. Period!

13. Longevity: The above arguments for 'commitment' apply to longevity, too. It is no longer a practical expectation. Points made for Teamwork and Dependence (5 and 16 respectively) also explain why longevity erodes due to people's inability to balance their rising needs for independence and dependence.

14. Financial Stability: An implied and important purpose of relationships is to force a degree of financial stability for the whole family's welfare. Partners must have adequate interest and knowledge to cooperate in managing their financial needs and long-term security, in particular by preventing waste and extravagance.

15. Compassion: Our ability to give and receive compassion is a direct function of our humanness and humility, which are becoming scarcer every year. Compassion depends on how good and enlightened a person is, as defined at the beginning of this chapter. Expecting compassion in relationships is a logical expectation, too. Yet, in reality, it rarely materializes at the desired and effective level, because everybody seeks more compassion every day, while the number of humble, patient people in the world is shrinking. Our superficial gestures of compassion, mostly through role-playing or even submission, cannot fill our need and craving for real compassion, either. People often detect our hypocrisy and resent it, mostly since we cannot play a natural role. Therefore, it is wise to set our expectations rather low for receiving adequate compassion in relationships, nowadays. But the question is whether we can fill this gap in our lives in some other way if relationships cannot fulfil our thirst for compassion? Need for compassion is too strong and urgent to ignore, after all. The answer is that we might, in fact, learn to play a major role personally in this matter, as will be suggested shortly.

The problem is that we always crave sympathy, but have difficulty expressing it ourselves. Usually we feel that our partners' needs are too superfluous and selfish. Compassion is demanded too often or partners' expectations seem insensible to each other. Sympathizing sincerely is tough, anyway, even when we feel that our partner's need for compassion is genuine. This is true, because most humans are inherently more selfish than compassionate.

Modern life's complexity is creating additional hardships and stress for everybody. Accordingly, demand for sympathy has increased astronomically. This is happening at the time when people are becoming more egotistical, impatient, and mentally too worn (because of their own problems and stress) to feel compassionate or provide sympathy to others. A person under constant pressure at work and from life conundrums is too preoccupied and exhausted to provide empathy to others, including his/her spouse. This is true, in particular, if his/her partner's demands are for satiating her/his deficiency need for attention. Partners are already playing enough games outside the house, so expecting them to use their exhausted brains to play similar games at home is simply impractical. Despite this obvious, persistent problem, marriage counsellors still keep advocating artificial means of expressing compassion in order to satiate partners' needs. On the top of the points noted above, the problem with this approach is that it would not be felt quite genuine by the receiver, and the giver loses the patience and interest to play games or roles.

Overall, people's need for sympathy is tremendously higher than we, as humans, are capable of delivering, especially in the new era. Thus, the supply and demand for compassion are drastically unbalanced in societies and across the nations. Yet, instead of recognizing this general shortfall of human nature, we take the matter personally and turn against our partners when they cannot give us as much compassion as we seek. We do not recognize our own inability to offer genuine sympathy often enough, but we are needy for it relentlessly. Nonetheless, compassion must be viewed in two dimensions as explained in the next two paragraphs.

On the one hand, couples must realize that expecting deep, authentic sympathy is unrealistic in a modern society where the supply and demand for compassion are quite unbalanced —mostly due to inherent human nature. Stress and depression have simply made us vulnerable and too needy for sympathy, but nobody out there is capable of giving it to us. Therefore, expecting it on a regular basis is both selfish and a definite cause for disappointment. Sympathy and compassion could (would) be exchanged naturally when people are capable and ready to express it. However, it leads to further alienation and resistance if it is demanded or perceived as an expectation. Receiving sympathy (and giving it) is a fringe benefit and not a right. Exchanging compassion is nice and helpful. It must be encouraged and appreciated. However, its inadequacy should not cause additional strain in relationships. Our partners might not be good in expressing compassion even if they genuinely mean to provide it. Conversely, learning to mimic compassion by reading a few books or attending seminars would never make people compassionate. If seeking phony compliments to satisfy our need for compassion, we will never fulfil our need for genuine compassion in relationships. We just keep asking for more love to feed our addiction to Elove and attention.

On the other hand, compassion is a reasonable expectation from relationships—with a major reservation in terms of its nature and source. A more realistic definition for compassion, nowadays, should mostly emphasize on our personal ability to generate it, instead of craving it. The best way to achieve this is by becoming a better person and supplying more compassion to others than demanding it. We must realize that *at best* we should expect compassion only if we are good at generating it ourselves. Needing something does not give us an entitlement to demand it. The big irony is that the more we learn to extend compassion sincerely, the higher our chance for receiving it from others becomes, and the less we feel the need for phony sympathies, anyway. By learning to become a compassionate person truly, we become self-sufficient largely and *possibly* get a lot of compassion in return, too. Therefore, in a sense, we can generate the compassion that we need personally. Only this mentality can reduce our depression and dependence on people and psychiatrists to manage our lives. Our need for compassion is too strong and urgent to ignore, after all.

Another crucial point is that, while compassion is an ideal personal attribute, knowing how to acknowledge, appreciate, and learn from, people's compassion towards us is even more urgent and important. We must know how to not only receive and return compassion, but also manage our lives personally, so that we are not so needy for compassion and other people's assistance as a way of living.

The bottomline is that everybody is alone in this world—an old saying that makes more sense every day, as we constantly adopt more egotism and individualism. Thus, we must define and manage our lives personally the best way within the hectic new societies. The point about our innate loneliness applies to the next relationship expectation (dependence) perfectly, too.

16. Dependence: Partners' efforts to align their needs for both dependence and independence create lots of inner conflicts for them and complicate their marriage. We get into relationships mostly for relieving our loneliness. We like to rely on a partner to make our lives easier. However, many relationships make partners feel the ultimate sense of loneliness, if not lots of new sources of pains, too. Maybe the sense of physical loneliness is remedied somewhat by living under the same roof with a partner. However, psychological loneliness increases quickly when partners fail to communicate. We feel the difficulty of relating to another person tangibly, because we had imagined we could understand her/him rather easily, mostly on the power of love alone. Most of us had probably never felt so helpless psychologically when we had been living alone. We are terribly disappointed after all the years of daydreaming about finding a partner to relieve our loneliness. Therefore, depending on our partners to cure our psychological loneliness is a rather unreasonable expectation.

Another big hurdle is that even if our partners were capable of satisfying our need for dependence, we personally sabotage their efforts by our juvenile expressions of individualism and independence. Our false pride prevents us from expressing our need for reliance on our partner's moral support naturally and directly. Instead, we keep pretending highly to be emotionally self-reliant. Showing our neediness could tilt the balance of power in relationship, after all.

Quite ironically, hiding their neediness to protect their pride cannot really help partners and their relationship, either! Only by sharing their emotions they can boost communication at least, if partners are mature enough to grasp marriage purposes and do not take advantage of each other's vulnerability.

Meanwhile, we strive to satisfy both our independence and dependence needs just by playing phony roles and expecting our partners to both understand their meanings and respond favourably. Yet, these conflicting (unexpressed) expectations and role-playing only frustrate our partners. They remember our previous shows of independence, especially when we play the role of a vulnerable partner seeking dependence swiftly. Showing the right balance of dependence and independence and clarifying the timing and issues on which we need our partners' support is difficult. We might imagine we are doing a good job of it, but that is only another selfish assumption and gross misperception.

Our struggles for independence and dependence make us jittery regularly. Therefore, we react unfavourably towards our partners, unjustifiably, especially when we assume they are refusing to recognize our needs intentionally. Naturally, when a partner seeks independence and finds his/her partner a big obstacle in achieving it, he/she feels frustrated and resentful towards him/her. And he/she gets frustrated, too, when he/she needs attention and dependence and his/her partner is not available or capable of providing it. The situation gets out of hand, since their relationship remains undefined in terms of partners' needs for dependency and independency. Partners' erratic attempts to be dependent or independent also confuse themselves, especially when they do not receive the responses they expect. While each partner has difficulty understanding and responding to his/her partner's incongruent expectations for dependence and independence, he/she is also frustrated when his/her own needs for dependence and independence remain unfulfilled.

These dual deprivations lead to personal (inner) conflicts for partners already. However, their inner conflicts heighten when their needs for dependence and independence do not coincide in terms of timing and partners' mood fluctuations. It hurts them deeply, since their natural (instinctual) personal needs for dependence and independence are badly imbalanced and ignored. This gross incongruity causes constant frictions between partners, while they also criticize each other's erratic needs. All along, partners' rotating struggles for more freedom or attention appear unnatural and sinister. The situation makes partners believe their partners are instable or neurotic. They also feel that their partners are placing these expectations on their relationship illogically or even out of spite. Thus, instead of grasping and *dealing with it logically*, they react negatively by further confrontations and retaliations. Thus, relationship mechanisms, including communication, stop working.

In all, it is difficult to deal with the unrealistic expectations of our partners for dependence and independence; especially in the eyes of an impatient partner who is unwilling or unable to cope with such conflicting needs (and demands) so often. The big irony is that people's needs for both independence and dependence are increasing simultaneously every day. As noted before, people are getting too spoiled and needy due to the effects of complex social values. They look for compassion (dependence), while also stress on their freedom and identity (independence). Of course, when partners accuse each other of erratic behaviour, they face only more arguments and anguish. Thus, instead of discussing their relationship dilemmas calmly and objectively, they focus only on dominating the situation and each other, or opt for separation. They see no option other than either adapting to this confusing environment or getting out of the relationship altogether. Both options are obviously destructive.

In our modern way of thinking, we accept open-mindedly that both dependence and independence are essential needs, and we naively believe we can cope with this major dilemma (conflict) in our marriages. We may even assume that we would find the right balance (between our needs for dependence and independence) by a magical power. We assume we can make enough compromises, so that both partners can satisfy their rotating needs for independence and dependence readily just through commonsense. This is a highly unrealistic expectation!

So, what is the solution? Since our emphasis, nowadays, is placed on individualism and independence, we must adjust our expectations from relationships accordingly. That is, **we must stick to independence and assume that relationships are no longer capable of satisfying our need for dependence at the desired level.** We must also prepare ourselves to deal with our inner conflicts (caused by inadequate support and dependence) without blaming our partners. Many readers might object: 'What is the point of being in a relationship if partners cannot depend on each other totally?' This is a valid question that is answered **fully** in the future chapters. However, the bottomline is that we cannot really demand independence so strongly and seek dependence randomly, too. This does not make real sense. Analysing this complex puzzle is this book's mission. We may still keep faith in our partners' integrity, cooperation, support, and sincerity, but certainly cannot demand total dependence. We must learn to be happy with a 'limited level of dependence conditional upon the overall health of our relationships,' but never total dependence. We should learn to accept this reality gracefully without making too much fuss or noise about it.

Again, **not fussing regarding dependence does not mean that partners do not advocate teamwork, compassion, and all the other good things that they must do together to make their relationship flourish.** Showing compassion helps the health (and dependency needs) of relationships whenever couples notice their partners' need for dependence despite their arrogant show of independence. It is a nice gesture by partners to stay civilized toward each other in those touchy conditions. However, when we keep switching between our independence roles and dependence urges erratically, we should also expect our partners lose their sensitivity and empathy about our needs. Meanwhile, partners' tensions rise, while they are unaware of the ongoing competition between their conflicting needs for independence and dependence. They feel only their partners' apathy toward their needs even when they play many idiotic roles themselves, including retaliation, to draw their attention.

Advocating independence in relationships might appear also inconsistent with the objective of 'enforcing teamwork.' However, 'teamwork' mostly entails an objective negotiation process between two independent partners, and not a sign of partners' dependence on each other.

Nonetheless, the options are clear: We could either keep looking for magical compromises, or agree on a practical set of principles that best fits the mentality of couples in modern societies. These principles, of course, lean towards partners' higher independence. The new trends indicate that couples consider independence their most urgent personal need, while give it the highest priority in their relationships. Accordingly, based on the strong trends evident in society, we must also emphasize that:

"Since we humans are usually unable to handle the rotating demands of our partners for independence and dependence, **we must adopt a relationship model** to handle the situation consistently. The increasing social fervour for independence suggests that, as a rule, couples should start with a relationship model that guarantees partners' independence. Thus, partners should reduce their expectations from relationships in terms of satisfying their dependence needs as well."

Accordingly, the relationship models discussed in Part III stress on partners' degree of independence and show how they also relate to relationships' success factors. Actually, partners' degree of independence provides the basis for setting all other expectations defined in Table 3.1 (Page 41). Now, our need for independence has become the locus of relationships, and thus it has affected all the expectations we had traditionally envisioned for relationships, especially financial security, i.e., the expectation number 2.

Whether we like it or not, we must adjust our assumptions about the conflicting needs of partners for both dependence and independence. It is time to stop the burdens of our useless struggles in relationships. These facts must be clear to couples at the outset before getting married. This is necessary because, nowadays, the old concept of 'dependence' has been losing its practicality in relationships. Thus, couples must think through and plan their relationships based on the assumption that they must remain mostly independent regardless of the outcome of their relationships. Let us hope partners learn teamwork and compromise, too, to make their relationships manageable and successful. However, starting on the wrong foot, i.e., hoping that their dependency need can be fulfilled in a relationship, is simply opening the door for major disappointments.

As noted before, the worst-case scenario erupts when one partner is really craving security and dependence upon his/her partner, but keeps playing the role of an independent person forcefully, while nagging about his/her partner's insensitivity, all at the same time. He/she does not admit that he/she is the one restricting his/her partner's ability to feel his/her need for dependence. He/she does not realize that his/her own rampant need for attention (and expecting his/her partner to sense it quickly and automatically, too) is frustrating his/her partner, as well as him/herself.

Based on the above analyses, and doing all the additions and deletions, Table 3.2 provides the updated list of relationship expectations for the new era.

Therefore, out of the eighteen general expectations from relationships, we can realistically consider only ten of them practical, nowadays, as marked by (X) in the right-hand-side column of Table 3.2 on the next page.

In the following chapters, this set of sensible expectations is applied to develop a relationship framework and a body of relationship principles. Surely, reducing our expectations from relationships feels like a major radical idea. However, partners must consider and implement this challenge along with other fundamental solutions noted in Chapter Eleven. Building this new mentality is crucial, if people are serious about improving the state of relationships. Radical solutions are only meant to facilitate partners' abilities to distinguish realistic expectations from unrealistic ones in line with contemporary social values. The essential goal is to introduce practical social mechanisms that support the hard process of partners' mental adjustment.

Table 3.2: The Updated List of Relationship Expectations

Type of Expectation	Delete Old	Add or Emphasize New	Sensible Expectations
1. Sex			X
2. Financial Security	X		
3. Communication		X	X
4. Companionship - Relate			X
5. Teamwork		X	X
6. SLove	X		
7. ELove	X		
8. MLove		X	X
9. Trust	X		
10. Happiness	X		
11. Friendship		X	X
12. Respect-Social acceptance		X	X
13. Personal Success		X	X
14. Commitment	X		
15. Longevity	X		
16. Financial Stability		X	X
17. Compassion			X
18. Dependence	X		

Chapter Four

Identifying Relationship Needs

An ideal relationship can *potentially* satisfy many of our basic, medium, and high-level needs. That is exactly why we crave love and a good companion. And that is exactly why we naively *perceive* 'relationship needs' as a natural extension of our 'personal needs.' These feelings and ensuing confusion are partly instinctual, but mostly the symptom of our phony social values making us too needy and desperate, while we also seek individualism and independence obsessively. Surely, placing such a high demand on relationships and society, to fulfil so many of our personal needs at all levels, is unrealistic. It is just making relationships and societies more chaotic and stressful. Our misperceptions regarding relationships per se (as discussed in Chapter Two), especially about love being the main success factor, deter our understanding of relationship needs altogether.

Some other implications are crucial to notice as well. First, the above facts actually emphasize the inherent significance of having a good companion. An ideal companion can seemingly resolve almost all of our problems and needs. Second, this psychological significance (and urgency) somewhat suggests that companionship must be viewed as a *basic* personal need, and not merely an extension of social (medium range) need.

This important viewpoint, and its impact on relationships, will be elaborated further in Chapter Ten.

Nevertheless, 'relationship needs' should supersede our 'personal needs' if we are really interested in the health of our relationships. We should learn to look at the bigger picture and stop fussing about our long list of artificial personal needs, especially love and trust. We must find ways of fulfilling our personal needs rather independently, so that the pressure on relationships is reduced.

We witness the sad facts about relationships, feel the heavy toll this situation is taking on our health, yet continue with our present approaches and mentalities. Why are we, as partners in this common cause, incapable of agreeing on a solution? Why do we actually sabotage the process of achieving our common objective, i.e., a manageable relationship, by humiliating and traumatizing our partners? Is it because we soon get tired of a relationship we had so eagerly tried to get into? Is it because partners' personal needs suffocate their relationship? Are our personal idiosyncrasies and insecurities getting out of control? Are too many philosophical slogans obscuring our sense of reality? Are our Ego and impatience stopping us from reaching a decent compromise? Is our sense of romanticism preventing us from assessing relationships' obstacles practically before marriage? Are not we intelligent enough? Are we hoping for miracles to save our relationships, instead of relying on proper principles to keep it together? Or is our legal system, which must strengthen the foundation of family life, actually hurting the situation? The answer is: All of the above.

Therefore, the first step is to discover those *specific needs of relationships* that can stir some harmony into relationships. The second step is to boost partners' willingness and patience to learn those needs. They should understand how relationship needs may clash with their personal needs. Furthermore, they should curb their Egos to stay objective. Many issues should be sorted out to make a relationship work, eh? Absolutely!

Nonetheless, we must learn to view 'relationships' as a unique entity with specific needs, which are totally different from the conflicting needs of the partners trying to run it. It is a pity our educational systems, especially at senior high school, do not devote a good portion of its required curriculum to this crucial real life subject.

Tables 4.1 and 4.2 reflect the results of discussions in the previous chapter and summarized in Table 3.2. Relationship needs can be developed around the list of valid relationship expectations (Table 4.1). Fulfilling these needs enhances the favorability of relationships. This list is not meant to be a final or complete list of relationship needs or success factors for relationships. Yet, it provides a solid working platform. The more favourable the factors in Table 4.1, the more successful a relationship would be. Many other factors could be identified and added to Table 4.1 later by researchers and scholars.

Table 4.1
Realistic Relationship Expectations

Realistic Relationship Expectations
1. Sex
2. Communication
3. Companionship - Relate
4. Teamwork
5. MLove
6. Friendship
7. Respect-Social acceptance
8. Personal Success
9. Financial stability
10. Compassion

Table 4.2
Unrealistic Relationship Expectations

Unrealistic Relationship Expectations
1. Financial Security
2. SLove
3. ELove
4. Trust
5. Happiness
6. Commitment
7. Longevity
8. Dependence

Of course, the unrealistic expectations in Table 4.2 materialize in some relationships automatically, too. Yet, they should be taken as fringe benefits of that particular relationship. The point is that couples must not view or start a relationship based on these invalid expectations, as they hardly materialize and last in relationships. This does not mean that their relationship is broken when they face the reality. Fulfilling the expectations in Table 4.1 even moderately would be a big success all by itself. With this mindset, partners would not blame each other for unfulfilled expectations or fuss too much about them.

The irony is that if couples fulfil the expectations listed in Table 4.1 effectively, the ones in Table 4.2 would most likely be satisfied automatically as well. They evolve gradually in their relationships based on partners' maturity. Once partners learn to live in peace with each other, love, happiness, and longevity would follow. But not if they keep thinking about, and pressing, on the invalid expectations in Table 4.2. In fact, pushing for the items in Table 4.2 hinders the fulfilment of the modest expectations in Table 4.1, and the relationship collapses under the pressures quickly. Enjoying companionship along with basic compassion should suffice without partners going overboard. That type of arrangement would prove fulfilling, anyway, because couples' invalid expectations do not distract them from the main goals of relationships.

The big hurdle, however, is that Ego and related emotions prevent people from staying content with a more realistic set of expectations. It looks bizarre when often a person starts to resent his/her partner and retaliates only because he/she feels that his/her partner does not love him/her enough! The basic question is how a person's love turns into hatred just because his/her partner cannot respond to his/her love. What kind of love had he/she had for his/her partner, anyway?

Relationship Purposes

The realistic purposes of relationships simply coincide with the expectations listed in Table 4.1 and discussed in Chapter Three. In fact, relationship needs, expectations, and purposes are almost identical. Meanwhile, the items in Table 4.2 might be viewed as **divine purposes** for only some blessed couples.

Oddly, most of us have never learned about the purposes of relationships due to our rising wild expectations during the last decades. We have trusted our imaginations and Egos to define them for us, so we often fail. The most crucial point, however, is that beyond its general purposes, the ultimate objective of relationships is to help couples face life's hardships together and reduce each other's burdens. Relationships might stir love and happiness, too, but not as a main purpose. An absence of adequate love or happiness in one's life is often only due to one's exaggerated expectations from life and relationships. The reason for so many relationship failures, nowadays, is that our present mentalities have developed wrongly with no real grasp of relationship purposes, especially the ultimate purpose of making life just a bit more endurable for partners. That is all!

Couples' Responsibilities

Although we must view relationships as an independent entity like a *romantic* business, the onus is still on partners to keep it functional, in the same way business partners and managers fulfil many responsibilities for keeping their business together. Couples must sacrifice even some of their personal needs, if necessary logically, to cope with and fulfil relationships' needs. Thus, 'Relationship Needs' and objectives refer to all the right things that partners should do for keeping their relationship healthy. Table 4.3 provides the list of 'Relationship Needs', which reflects Couples' Responsibilities (and success factors) for satisfying the relationship expectations listed in Table 4.1 and boosting their relationships' health.

Table 4.3: Basic Relationship Needs for the New Era
(Partners' Responsibilities for Building a Successful Relationship)

1. Relationship needs consist of partners' basic responsibilities for fulfilling the sensible expectations in Table 4.1. They are in line with relationships' main purposes in order to give their relationship a good chance for success.

2. Accordingly, Relationship Needs, Relationship Purposes, Partners' Responsibilities, and Relationship Success Factors have the same (or interrelated) implications in line with the points outlined in this Table.
3. Partners learn to view their relationship as an independent entity (R-entity) that has specific needs, which are different from their personal needs.
4. Partners realize their responsibilities for fulfilling the unique Relationship Needs listed here, instead of relying on (and expecting) their relationship to satisfy their personal needs.
5. Partners distinguish relationships' realistic expectations from unrealistic ones. Then, they discuss and agree to focus only on the realistic expectations from their relationship.
6. Partners keep their expectations within the boundary noted in Table 4.1.
7. Partners know the repercussions of pushing the expectations in Table 4.2.
8. Partners give their relationship needs the highest priority as a sacred foundation for building a friendly environment free from dogmatism and pressures.
9. Partners are attracted to each other physically somewhat at least, but mostly *stay in tune* emotionally and intellectually.
10. Partners have chosen a relationship model suitable for their personalities. Relationship Models are discussed in Part III. Mainly, relationship models' purpose is to clarify partners' means of relating. The goal is to align partners' needs for dependence and independence in line with modern world's zeal for individualism. Choosing the right relationship model and agreeing on it at the outset is vital for facilitating their communication. Surely, the smart thing to do, nowadays, is to set the practical level of dependence based on partners' seeming dependability and long-term behaviour and not their words—although this is a difficult mission with still no guarantees! We cannot always keep their promises simply

due to limitations in our own lives and psyches, and not necessarily out of malice or spite.

11. Partners maintain a high degree of personal integrity when dealing with each other.
12. Partners are mentally prepared to leave their relationship peacefully when reconciliation is not possible.
13. Partners contemplate teamwork, instead of retaliation, for convincing each other about something.
14. Partners strive to remain tactful, mature, forgiving, patient, and sensible.
15. Partners do not play games with each other.
16. Partners do not need, nor rely on, government or religion to regulate and run their relationship.
17. Partners deem separation a normal expectation, nowadays.
18. Partners believe in terminating their relationships civilly if necessary.
19. Partners have signed a contract at the outset to govern their financial and marital duties, especially during separation.
20. Partners assess and discuss their relationship state regularly.
21. Partners strive to remain mostly independent financially and emotionally within their relationship model's requirements, as they cooperate to draw proper family plans and budgets.
22. Partners know that, beyond people's *instinctual urge,* they seek independence in the new era, because they: (1) have become too obsessed with individualism and asserting their identities, (2) should strive to cope with social norms and be accepted, and, (3) finally learn they cannot rely on others.
23. Partners know that the purpose of choosing a relationship model is to help them relate more effectively and handle many personal inner conflicts that relationships cause. They realize that each partner must deal with his/her dilemma of dependence versus independence personally, as explained in the following three distinct ways:
    - He/she must initially try to establish his/her realistic needs for dependence and independence, only based on his/her

personality without considering any compromises needed for being in any serious relationship with a partner. The objective is to establish one's true temperament and needs regardless of social pressures for independence or the level of compromise necessary in a particular relationship.

- He/she must envision and set the levels of independency/dependency he/she can bear for any prospective partner. Often people dislike partners who crave independence. More worrying, however, is when a person is unprepared (perhaps psychologically) or unwilling to be responsible for a partner who seeks lots of dependence (emotionally or financially). Therefore, he/she should figure out his/her potential partner's tendency for dependence/independence realistically before committing him/herself to a particular relationship model.
- Together with his/her potential partner, they should set the kind of dependency/independency levels they require in their relationship. This balance should fit the other two above decisions that each partner makes personally first, then they choose the best relationship model accordingly.

24. Partners are able to relate rather actively, regardless of the relationship model (and independence level) they choose.
25. Partners have rather compatible lifestyles and preferences.
26. Partners stay within their relationship model's boundaries.
27. Partners pursue a basic self-awareness routine to detect their personal idiosyncrasies that may damage their relationship.
28. Partners pursue a path of self-awareness also for enhancing their sense of self-reliance, individualism, Self, SLove, and personal search for self-fulfilment and compassion.
29. Partners know the meaning and repercussions of egotistical demands for love and attention. They know how to depend on Mlove, respect, and courtesy to spread a civilized sense of love and cooperation between them. They also know the meaning and implications of ELove, MLove, and SLove.

30. Partners know how everybody's personality is shaped and controlled by forces beyond his/her control. Two damaging misperceptions in relationships are that, i) our partners are in control of their personalities, and ii) they can change themselves easily. Therefore, we rush to retaliate in our own ways in order to teach them a lesson. We ignore the fact that retaliations only add more barriers for couples to assess the viability of their relationships objectively.
31. Partners grasp and negate the lure of varied misperceptions, including the ones noted in # 30 above, that confuse and hinder communications. Misperceptions have many natures. Generally, however, they usually result from partners' ego, carelessness, oversensitivity, or impatience.
32. Partners understand the inherent flaws of human nature and how they contaminate relationships.
33. Partners do not keep criticizing each other's idiosyncrasies.
34. Partners do not strive to change each other or impose their lifestyles on each other.
35. Partners strive sincerely to develop trust and dependence between them, but do not make an issue about the overall level of trust and dependence in their relationship.
36. Partners do not manipulate, control, or intimidate each other.
37. Partners know how to maintain good communication.
38. Partners enjoy having sex together and do not withdraw this basic need for retaliation and blackmail.
39. Partners run their family responsibilities through teamwork.
40. Partners are compassionate and know how to show passion and compassion through MLove. They also know how to acknowledge and appreciate the compassion they receive.
41. Partners are good friends. They know the rules, boundaries, and benefits of friendship and stick to them.
42. Partners know that people's (including their partner's) flaws limit their abilities to perceive things and behave logically, let alone ideally. They use this knowledge to enhance their own compassion and patience in their relationship.

43. Partners respect each other, despite their partner's irritating idiosyncrasies.
44. Partners are capable of grasping and promoting each other's needs for independence and dependence.
45. Partners can support each other in pursuing their personal goals and social ambitions.
46. Partners are aware how their imposing personality aspects (i.e., Ego, Model, and Self) interfere during their encounters and watch their effects closely.
47. Partners appreciate the purpose, principles, and components of the Relationship Framework (as discussed in Part II).
48. Partners adopt the Relationship Framework and follow its guidelines actively.
49. Partners realize the need for, and actively follow, a reliable set of relationship principles, such as the ones suggested in Chapter Seven. They use these principles to stay objective in their relationship and minimize the chances of anger and Ego tainting their judgments and decisions. They seek expert advice and mediation when disagreements arise.
50. Partners have enough financial knowledge and sense to not only cooperate in securing the required financial resources, but also avoid waste and extravagance to goad a long-term plan for their marriages' financial stability.

A more complete list of 'relationship needs' (success factors) must be built soon after deeper analyses and contributions of scholars. These relationship needs would also provide the foundation for developing the detailed relationship principles that are discussed in Chapter Seven.

PART II

Relationship Framework

Chapter Five

The Transition

Let us hope the readers agree by now that humans need a solid relationship framework to face the sad realities noted in Part I. Nevertheless, relationships will continue to go through a long, painful transition in the 21st century with unpredictable (mostly ominous) outcome. We have the option of making this transition smoother towards a more thoughtful and acceptable relationships setting or just wait and let it grow through chaos, which would most likely raise social unrest and stress, too. The future of family and social health is in great jeopardy. The result depends on our success to revamp our mindsets, develop a modern relationship framework, and introduce a bunch of radical social mechanisms compatible with couples' modern lifestyles and drive for individualism. Otherwise, we are all doomed, especially the new generations. This is not a cynical or naive opinion, either! I promise! Any objective person can see this prospect, which is almost as catastrophic and urgent as climate crisis.

Of course, developing and propagating a viable relationship framework would be a tough job. Even defining its parameters would be hard, since such a framework must be quite flexible to accommodate a large variety of couples' personalities. In addition, it must be justifiable as a novel, practical approach to relationships with valid objectives. It should make sense to highly dogmatic people around the world, especially to those living in progressive societies. It sounds like an impossible job, and the author is the first person to admit that. Yet, we can overcome all these hurdles if only we change our mentalities about relationships and see the need for a framework.

The ideal would have been to amalgamate all the effective ideas that relationships experts are using these days into one comprehensive, easy to understand document. Our inability to do this task easily merely proves that marital solutions presently suggested by scholars and marriage counsellors are impotent, incompatible, and not universally accepted.

Anyway, the simple fact remains that without a framework, the state of relationships will deteriorate beyond control very soon. It will reach a highly explosive and unmanageable level. Sooner or later, we will be forced to acknowledge that some kind of a framework is needed, so that we can measure and manage our relationships more objectively. So, we might as well get serious now. If we begin working on it now, we may have a reasonably practical framework in place within the next few decades or so. However, we would all benefit from this work in progress a lot immediately, as soon as we adopt a new mentality about relationships. We must merely believe in the need for such a framework and then continue to work on its development seriously and systematically. The objectives of the relationship framework are discussed in the remainder of this chapter and then the benefits and means of promoting this project are explained in the future chapters.

Objectives of a Relationship Framework

The main objectives of a relationship framework are to:

A. Enforce teamwork.
B. Bring objectivity back into relationships.
C. Increase the effectiveness of communications.

D. Reduce partners' expectations from relationships as much as necessary in order to create the right balance between their personal needs and the relationship needs.
E. Overhaul individuals' mentalities and social mechanisms regarding relationships.

Discussing the merits and goals of a relationship framework without knowing what a 'relationship framework' looks like might annoy some readers. So, a couple of points must be made in advance. First, although a preliminary format for a relationship framework will be suggested in the following chapters, developing its final form is not a task for this book. It will take many years before such a framework can be fully developed. Second, a relationship framework has many parts and components, as discussed in Chapter Six. It is better to define those components first and then let the framework evolve by itself through these discussions. At least, this is the approach followed in this book. Nonetheless, convincing the readers about the *need* for a relationship framework—*why* and *how* it can help couples—is the most crucial task. Modifying people's mentalities about relationships is the most vital step. So, this chapter provides more details about the objectives of a relationship framework, and then the following chapters will explain its format, components, principles, and characteristics.

Objective A: Enforce teamwork

Teamwork is not a revolutionary idea or a concept forgotten by couples, but actually being committed to it, as the sole solution for relationships, is a different thing. Commitment to teamwork is hard, especially, while couples strive for individualism and independence so obsessively. Indeed, partners often perceive teamwork and individualism as two contradictory concepts. They misperceive 'compromising' as an infringement on their individualism. Their partners' suggestions come across as a deliberate opposition or an intrusion of their independence. This is how our Egos regularly operate. Thus, a relationship framework should somehow overcome all these obstacles and prove the merits of real teamwork. The challenge is to invent the means of enforcing teamwork principles without offending partners' perception of their individuality. The radical solutions suggested in Chapter Eleven would accomplish this objective largely, as partners would find it to their advantage to partake in teamwork naturally.

A big hurdle, nowadays, is that couples often do not know the meaning of compromise, or the method or timing to make one. Sometimes partners compromise just to show their sense of cooperation. They usually do this untimely or for a wrong reason. For example, a person needs his/her partner's objective and honest opinion to make the best decision together, but his/her partner simply agrees with him/her casually or maybe even callously. This partner ignores, or is unaware of, the process of reaching a compromise. S/he only pretends to do it merely for showing his/her cooperation, or simply because he/she has no courage to take the risk of expressing his/her opinion, e.g., about certain investment. Then, this same partner makes a big fuss if the outcome of that decision (or compromise) turns out poorly. S/he tries to dissociate him/herself from the wrong decision. S/he declares his/her initial input merely a gesture of support rather than consent. Overall, partners often lose their opportunities to benefit from each other's wisdom, since they are incapable of discussing the pros and cons of their plans calmly through teamwork. Other times, couples compromise simply because a partner is showing so much sensitivity (or resistance) towards a specific suggestion only out of spite or narrow-mindedness. Therefore, one partner gives in, because reasoning has stopped working.

The ever-increasing need for individuality is a given fact in relationships. Accordingly, teamwork is facing the highest level of resistance by partners, due to their obsession for some crude perception of independence. They do not see that teamwork is actually the only tool that might guarantee their independence, not arguments and retaliations. Enforcing such mentality in relationships would be hard. And that is exactly the reason 'teamwork' is a main parameter of a relationship framework. It will take many decades for couples to change their mindsets and accept teamwork as a major requirement for boosting both their independence and relationships. Yet, it must happen soon to minimize havoc in relationships.

Obviously, there is no need to emphasize on the merits of teamwork in any environment. Rather, the objective is to stress that: For the simple reason that individuality is becoming the most important requirement of relationships, developing new methods of teamwork is imperative more than ever, nowadays. New methods of teamwork might depend on a variety of tools, e.g., a simple agreement for sharing family responsibilities and finances and sticking to the plan.

A vital role of teamwork is to keep partners' personal needs aligned with the relationship needs based on the relationship model they chose. It was explained why couples' expectations from their relationships must be reduced in order to align their personal needs and relationship needs. Lots of teamwork is in particular required to maintain this fine balance and remain within the relationship model's boundaries they have chosen.

Still another role of teamwork would be to abolish the need for equality struggles. People's misperceptions about equality (for stirring major relationship conundrums) were discussed on page 31. Once partners learn to concentrate on teamwork, their obsession for *equality* subsides. Instead of depending on equality, or superiority, the success of relationships would be measured merely by the smooth operation and outcome of teamwork—not partners' level of influence over each other.

Indeed, the strength of teamwork lies on its emphasis on partners' independence and objectivity. Their independent (yet objective) opinions are needed for important family decisions.

This is more in line with the new trend in society to promote individualism. Yet, it also gives partners a chance to use their unique expertise for the benefit of their relationship without being constantly second-guessed by their partners. Partners' roles are clearest in teamwork. This is contrary to the existing approach where partners are confused or depressed about their roles, because they are mostly preoccupied by equality games. It is indeed too difficult to understand the equality rules, since we have not yet established the objectives and means of *family equality*. Equality, and measuring it, remains ambiguous and arbitrary at best. It lives only in people's imaginations and it manifests in the form of immature games of resistance and confrontation with no definite purpose or guideline.

Everybody is deeply paranoid about fairness these days. Therefore, the relationship framework should replace the need for couples' constant struggle for equality. By insisting on *equality* in all aspects of relationships, couples are wasting energy on measuring every activity or incident subjectively, instead of focusing on teamwork objectively. The flexibility of a universal framework could replace the rigidity of equality approach and create synergy within relationships, too.

Relationships thrive when couples adopt complementary roles, while giving each other room to act independently. They do not need to fight for inequality, unfairness, independence, etc. A relationship framework would facilitate both teamwork and partners' independence. While men and women have the same rights and acknowledge each other's contributions, they need not share the same tasks and roles to ensure equality. This is an obvious concept, but in reality couples waste a lot of energy these days consciously and subconsciously, on gauging the difficulty of various responsibilities and quarrelling about them. Presently, nobody knows enough about the mechanisms of a reliable relationship framework, while many imaginary notions about relationships confuse couples.

The best test of equality about partners' decision making or sharing household affairs is to see how well their activities and ideas fit within the guidelines (spirit) of teamwork. If they do not fit, they are biased, Ego driven, and futile. On the contrary, understanding the spirit of teamwork and implementing it in relationships would enhance partners' Self and Model at the expense of Ego—thus more effective relationships. Overall, teamwork guidelines would inherently ensure couples' fairer treatment of each other, which is the goal of equality struggles theoretically. By adhering to some preliminary guidelines for relationships (and teamwork), partners' rights would be best served in a setting built for coexistence. Thus, the question is, if some standards can be invented to maximize the benefits of teamwork in relationships what would they look like? This question is addressed in the future chapters.

Considering the vast power of teamwork, it is astonishing how our Ego prevents Self and Model to play a more direct role in relationships and make teamwork a more successful mechanism. Thus, a crucial goal of the relationship framework is to ***enforce*** teamwork. The relationship framework's format is such that teamwork cannot be bypassed.

Objective B: Bring objectivity back into relationships

Objectivity has been eroded in relationships, nowadays, due to couples' growing Egos and expectations. Instead, relationships are now misperceived as a mechanism to fulfil a large variety of partners' personal needs.

In the author's opinion, objectivity was more defined and achievable a few decades ago, because relationship goals were limited, manageable, and better understood. Those objectives fell more in line with humans' traditional and instinctual needs to cooperate for building a family. This preliminary principle worked better even for our Stone Age ancestors, but not any longer. Now, a large array of artificial expectations, including the endless demands for compassion, independence, love, and extravagance, burdens relationships. In line with our personal obsession for more affection and materials, we have reduced relationships' capacity to be objective. Furthermore, partners have different ideas regarding the type and level of personal needs that their relationship should satisfy. At the same time, our obsession for having a soul mate has never been so high, while we also trust one another very little, and while need for a companion has emerged as an urgent need of people in the new era. The relationships setting has never been so complex, yet least objective.

In all, couples' subjective perceptions of relationships and their unrealistic demands have made the mission of managing relationships quite difficult for couples. Therefore, to reduce family clashes, we must somehow bring objectivity back into relationships by creating a practical relationship framework and viewing relationships as an independent entity separate from couples' personalities.

Relationships are supposed to create synergy when couples combine their resources, especially their brains, effectively. Often, however, the opposite happens when retaliations bring couples' lives to a halt. Instead of empowering each other, partners often compete and retaliate. A reason for conflicts in relationships is that couples keep arguing about the roles they like to play, either independently or jointly. Each partner likes to set the rules for their relationship. This decision is usually according to his/her rotating and abrupt preference to push his/her *need for independence*, (e.g., making investment or some family decisions alone), or *need for dependence*, (e.g., seeking support and attention). One goal of a relationship framework is to eliminate conflicts caused by partners' extreme, erratic need changes or equality arguments. The modest guidelines of a framework could replace couples' arbitrary and emotional decision processes in relationships. Clearly, synergy is usually achieved better when partners work together to fulfil certain tasks or share decision-making needs of a relationship. Yet, synergy can also be achieved if couples support each other to perform their specific roles with independence.

The new framework can help (and rather force) couples set their objectives and expectations from relationships somewhat realistically. The framework gives couples the opportunity of settling their conflicts objectively, considering all the inevitable emotional episodes in relationships. Moreover, it will increase objectivity by identifying a handful of relationship models that can fit a large variety of individuals' personalities, while each model provides the main advantages of being in a relationship. The ultimate goal is to minimize arguments about every task or issue and to reduce couples' urges for aggressive behaviour when they feel some kind of unfairness. All these steps would enhance relationships' objectivity.

In recent decades, relationships' success is gauged only by partners' feelings. Although partners' impressions and feelings matter a lot, they do not reflect whether their relationship failed due to partners' extreme expectations, oversensitivity, or real lack of compatibility. Nowadays, we rely on partners to assess their relationship subjectively, as no definition for a successful relationship exists. Two partners in a particular relationship might indeed rate their relationship's success quite differently. This is because they are biased and mostly act based on their raw emotions. Furthermore, this type of assessment lacks any basis to compare different relationships against one another and find universally agreeable rules and anomalies. Couples' assessments of their own relationships reveal one interesting fact, though: that most relationships are failures if we asked couples to rate them. This is because almost nobody is happy with his/her relationship these days. Seldom both partners see their relationship a success. Even then, they are probably using wrong or biased criteria for measuring its success.

Another reason for partners' negative impressions of their relationships and the loose definition of 'relationship success' in general is that people's expectations from relationships have grown too fast beyond anybody's capacity to respond to. This situation surely cannot continue forever. As noted repeatedly, relationship expectations are rising due to the rampant increase in couples' personal needs and social push for extravagance. People imagine some phony lifestyle or ideals, which they impose on their relationships, too. This conceited attitude has raised the bar for relationship success, as partners' expectations have become larger than the sum of all the expectations that people have imitated from one another and the movies. That is, everybody likes to have everything that all other couples *seem to enjoy* in their relationships plus everything else that their own imaginations suggest. Instead of gauging the success of relationships objectively, we merely let the selfishness and neediness of partners make this critical judgment. Therefore, only the degree of their arrogance is being measured, and not the success of their relationship. Surely, this open-ended level of expectations from relationships cannot prevail forever if we care about a healthy social environment. The faster these crude expectations escalate, the less successful relationships become (appear to people).

With our rampant needs for things, sympathy, and security, we are also placing a lot of pressure on society and limiting relationships' chances of following a practical path. In return, the impact of the failing relationships is depressing individuals and society as a whole, too, which then again stirs up people's mistrust, but also their urge for more compassion. This vile, complex cycle is feeding and forcing itself out of control. We must somehow deal with this situation before the time comes when everybody needs antidepressants in order to go through a day. We must redefine relationships as an independent entity with unique needs and remember that relationship expectations beyond some modest, humanistic level are too whimsical and imposed by mentally distressed, deprived people.

Partners should monitor the relationship needs (success factors) that were discussed in Part I. More urgently, however, they must learn to disallow superficial criteria (their subjective judgments) obscure their views of their relationships. It means less imposition of their personal needs on their relationship and less hasty judgments of each other based on their personal crooked expectations. Neither idealism nor idiosyncrasies of partners must overwhelm their relationship. Now, we need a *relationship framework* that enforces partners' objectivity mostly by aligning their personal needs and relationship needs.

Objective C: Increase communication effectiveness

The effectiveness of partners' communications has declined drastically, since they have become too emotional, subjective, Ego driven, and destructive. This deficiency is causing many relationship conflicts and the situation will continue to worsen unless couples are given better tools for communicating and relating more effectively. The goal is to minimize the effect of partners' Egos during family discussions, although it is a rather unrealistic expectation. Obviously, we can never eliminate bad communications and arguments, especially when one or both partners are too selfish or mentally sick. Yet, a relationship framework provides enough guidelines to reasonably logical couples to negotiate within certain boundaries and minimize the chances of miscommunication. It would give partners a chance to make their communications mostly goal-oriented in a teamwork setting. This improved objectivity would reduce Ego somewhat and minimize arguments by stressing more on partners' autonomy.

A major flaw in our approach towards relationships is that we usually examine a relationship only when it is in trouble. Otherwise, it is taken for granted the way our ancestors did intuitively. Driven by our traditional mindset, we still assume (and expect) that relationships would keep working smoothly as a routine social arrangement. However, then, relationships were defined by simple cultural rules and they remained safe inherently without the need for so much communication. In progressive societies, however, relationships require constant communication and they are extremely vulnerable from day one, because a great deal of juvenile jargons and expectations has complicated the workings of relationships. Accordingly, partners cannot comprehend or respond to relationship needs intuitively. Actually, they cannot detect the real sources of relationship problems even when they attempt to explore them actively. Not even relationship experts and counsellors can help couples in most cases. The irony is that most often the problems are simply due to partners' naïveté about the purpose and potentials of relationships, as their criteria is vastly tainted by superficial needs and social imitations. Most relationships would have been considered acceptable if couples were not so grossly misled by superficial lifestyles, misperceptions, and miscommunications. For this reason alone, sadly, now couples' struggles to salvage their relationships usually proves futile, despite all the efforts that partners and relationship counsellors put into them. Partners just do not know how to communicate in a timely and proper manner even regarding basic issues, let alone about the rising relationship conflicts.

Objective D: Reduce our expectations from relationships

The fourth objective of a relationship framework is to keep partners' expectations low in general, even with regard to the sensible ones listed in Table 4.1. They should reduce them as much as necessary until their personal and relationship needs are aligned. They must impose and respect certain boundaries around their ideals regarding the capacity of relationships to provide all the good things they imagine it can provide in line with all personal ambitions they envision. For one thing, we value our identity and independence above our relationships, while raising our demands more from our relationships in all respects as well, nowadays. Yet, at the same time, we have been placing more demands on relationships. For example, we expect our partners and relationships to bring us happiness and lots of compassion on the top of love. This is unrealistic, since the logic dictates that the more we seek independence, the less we like to rely on others, and the less we must expect from our relationships, too. We must become more self-reliant to boost our independence and individuality.

Couples must always remember that their personal needs and relationship needs are not the same or coincidental. Every relationship consists of two people with different personalities and perceptions. Thus, their conflicting personal needs cause relationship clashes regularly. Especially, while both partners insist on individualism, the areas of common interest between them decline drastically. Each partner gives priority to his/her personal needs and his/her perceived big expectations from an imaginary relationship. Accordingly, they cannot comply with the particular needs of relationships, either, even if they knew what they were.

Ideally, partners must have the will and knowledge to lower their expectations from their relationship, if they really wish to keep it. In practice, however, it is difficult to expect this kind of understanding and sacrifice, especially from young couples. Thus, a relationship framework is needed to do it for them, i.e., to reconcile couples' personal needs with the relationship needs in a logical and proactive manner.

A useful relationship framework should have a flexible structure to accommodate a big variety of personalities, while partners try to revamp their perceptions of relationships, too. Surely, this framework would not satisfy all the personal needs and expectations of couples. It can fulfil *somewhat* only a bunch of sensible needs that are most commonly agreeable to the public—just enough to make relationships bearable, and a chance for more. However, these global needs would most likely do not include many of personal needs of couples, e.g., love or happiness—as much as they would have desired from an imaginary relationship.

In all, the relationship framework has no mandate to stir happiness, nor can it respond to partners' crude preferences for an ideal relationship. Consequently, couples' personalities and perceptions must not besiege their relationships. Partners can learn slowly that pursuing the basic guidelines of a framework might give their relationship a better chance to survive. It also provides the right atmosphere for smart partners to look for happiness individually first and then possibly together as well. Most of all, couples learn that they cannot (and should not) depend on their relationships to fulfil all their personal needs, especially happiness.

Partners might not like all the features of this framework, but adopting it would be better than arguing with their partners all the time or living alone. Since all relationships would be following the same guidelines, no one would feel oppressed in a particular relationship. Partners also know that going to a different relationship would not change the rules of the game. People would judge all relationships and their success merely based on couples' abilities to adhere to the general guidelines of the relationship framework. Partners get into relationships with advance knowledge of the rules of the game. If they do not like the framework, they should not start a relationship, unless both partners agree to have a relationship arrangement outside this global framework. Thus, couples would still have a choice to set their relationships outside the norms set by the general relationship framework if they desired to do so. Yet, for the majority of us, sticking to a general framework would prove more practical and effective in the long run.

A major purpose of developing a framework is to discuss and eliminate many of the existing misperceptions regarding relationships. Once we have a better appreciation of what does not work anymore in the new era, we can set out to create a viable framework and mindset. Ultimately, we are forced to reduce our expectations from relationships drastically whether we like or not, so with might as well do it by choice through personal initiatives.

Objective E: Overhaul couples' mentalities and social mechanisms

As evident from the discussions in this chapter, a great deal of soul searching and mental adjustments is needed in order to adapt our relationships to the new social framework. We need radical changes in our mentalities, and we must change social mechanisms, especially the legal system, to fit our personal needs and lifestyles in modern societies. These topics, as well as some solutions, are discussed in Chapter Eleven.

The Ultimate Objective of a Relationship Framework

The *ultimate, sacred* objective for adopting the 'relationship framework' is to make as many relationships *manageable* as possible by pursuing objectives A through E noted above. Even imperfect relationships have some merits if couples learn to relate (at least passively) by choosing a relationship model suitable for their needs and personalities. Dreaming about an ideal relationship is merely a waste of our precious lives. Only by curbing our imaginations about the potentials and purposes of relationships we might be able to boost teamwork and find mechanisms to manage our marriages better. For this sacred goal, we need a relationship framework compatible with our modern lifestyles.

In the old times, relationships were not as much important, understood, or perfect. Couples had simply learned to cope with the limitations of relationships and did not jump out of them when they were not perfect. They had more tolerance naturally because their brains were not washed with imaginary notions about relationships. They were not obsessed with love or an idealistic perception of relationships. Now, everything has changed. Especially, three clashing conditions are making life unbearable for everybody: 1) Relationships have become vastly complex, 2) we crave the opportunity of having a soul mate more than ever, and 3) we have become too demanding, arrogant, and impatient.

Surely, we all need a companion with certain qualities and mutual attraction. The problem is that the lack of discipline in relationships has ruined our chances to ponder and follow this matter logically. The problem is not as much in finding good mates as it is in keeping them, as people's traditional tolerance in relationships has been replaced by oversensitivity and high expectations, nowadays. The reasons behind people's rising impatience are noted throughout this book. However, social stress, our increasing need for individualism, romanticism, loss of trust, and thirst for love and respect are to be blamed. In addition, we have become more snotty, spoiled, idealistic, demanding, choosy, and ignorant about the acceptable level of tolerance in relationships.

In all, our naïve perceptions regarding social realities have made life unbearable for everybody and the situation would get even worse if a solution is not found soon. Recognizing the real potentials of relationships in present culture is crucial for cleansing our wild imaginations. Simply, relationships are incapable of providing all the niceties that we have gradually turned into relationship expectations in recent decades. Now, we have created merely more deprivation for ourselves by our wild views about relationship potentials, especially in terms of bringing us love and happiness.

Therefore, another objective of a relationship framework is to make us contemplate on life and relationship realities a bit more realistically. It would also give us a chance to develop a rational measure of the acceptable level of tolerance gradually.

This objectivity about tolerance level should replace couples' subjective judgments or crooked senses of romanticism to guess the level of reasonable tolerance. Of course, each couple determines their tolerance level for their unique circumstance. However, they also have access to a more realistic standard of tolerance in society to avoid gross misperceptions. Choosing between relationships with general imperfections and isolation is a tough task and requires an objective sense for acceptable tolerance level. The question is if we prefer to live in a fantasy world and dream about a rather perfect relationship or learn about reducing our expectations largely. Our options seem to be clear. They are:

- Keep fighting with our partners and ourselves forever over the irreconcilable issues of relationships in the new era, or live in solitude, while sticking to some rigid perceptions of an ideal relationship.
- Learn to accept the reality of modern relationships and their vast hassles, reduce our expectations from them, fulfil as much of our personal needs outside our relationships as necessary without tainting their sanctities, tolerate a rather irritable mate, cope with inevitable relationship hardships, and separate peacefully when it proves unmanageable.

The *ultimate* objective of a relationship framework and this book's discussions is to advocate the second option. This book is less useful to people who prefer the first option. However, a bigger purpose of a relationship framework is to prevent the start of doomed relationships based on customary unrealistic expectations. The objective is to stop couples from wasting their lives in torturous relationships if they cannot reduce their expectations at the outset. The guidelines of the relationship framework can actually help those couples with unrealistic expectations, too, because they get the opportunity of raising them directly at the outset and discussing them. Conversely, a relationship framework can also help people overcome their fears of getting into relationships and facing their headaches, since ending them would be less hectic in the new legal setup —something that we can demand and hope to materialize in a society that seems to have no interest to resolve the roots of social issues. For now, we might at least ponder the likelihood and benefits of some form of sensibility being injected into relationships by propagating a viable relationship framework.

Ultimately, a relationship framework seems to be the only mechanism to *enable partners relate to each other effectively and efficiently* even when many of their personal expectations cannot be fulfilled in their relationship. In that environment, a better sense of reality along with higher standards of behaviour and communication can help partners *relate* somehow, maybe even somewhat passively if necessary, with minimal frictions and stress. The goal is to develop a self-sustaining mechanism to gauge couples' means of relating to each other on a regular basis.

The first step, of course, is for both partners to imagine and agree that: A relationship is an *independent* setting, and not a collection of partners' untamed expectations (from each other and their relationship). Then, they can learn about the format of a framework that defines and supports the unique needs of this independent entity—relationships. The main assumption is that working from within this framework gives partners a better chance to communicate and relate. This means they agree on the relationship needs listed in Table 4.3 and learn to follow some specific guidelines to *relate* to each other, instead of hoping for it to happen automatically or by a lifelong trial and error.

Chapter Six

Relationship Framework's Components

We all imagine intuitively that some special factors can help relationships flourish better. It also makes sense to let a set of modest standards and principles define the parameters for the success of relationships in modern societies, instead of letting couples depend merely on their whims or other people's crude opinions. This basic intuition implies that we already perceive relationships as an independent *entity* with unique needs and characteristics. This means 'relationships' should be free from partners' erratic judgments and perceptions about happiness, love, and similar ideals that merely mislead couples. Couples' personalities and perceptions must not interfere and besiege their relationships constantly. Accordingly, a crucial question always boggling partners' minds is, "What factors make a relationship successful or a failure?"

We make statements like, "They have a good relationship; they can relate; or this relationship is doomed, etc." On these occasions, we somehow perceive a 'relationship' as a setting, with particular characteristics and needs. Obviously, the health of any relationship depends mostly on couples' capacities and personalities, including partners' mentalities, their abilities for relating to one another, their grasps of the relationship needs, their patience, etc. However, we perceive 'relationships' as a state of affairs between partners, which could be good, bad, or whatever, based on tangible factors. For example, if partners argue a lot or are depressed about the way things are going in their personal or joint life, then their relationship is rated low.

Thus, the first step for assessing relationship conflicts is to establish whether the problems are genuine or the figments of partners' unrealistic expectations, quirks, oversensitivity, or unfulfilled personal needs. The outcome might not change if partners cannot live together for whatever reasons. However, we would at least know whether the problems are within or outside the acceptable boundaries of a normal relationship. We would know whether those problems are imaginary or real, based on partners' erroneous assumptions or even mental illness in some respect. Many relationships are ruined these days simply because one or both partners underestimate the value of their relationship prematurely. If they had objective criteria to measure the health of their relationship, maybe it could have been saved. They might have realized that they must face the problems realistically rather than running away to find a better relationship, or merely out of spite. The onus should be placed on partners to establish the validity of their expectations from relationships. It is time to realize that letting relationship expectations escalate forever in line with couples' rising personal needs is an absurd, doomed social norm. This approach would only lead to major socioeconomic suffering around the globe.

Thus, we need a progressive and proactive environment to goad couples see their options more clearly at least, and then choose a proper approach for assessing the state and success of their relationships. It must help them adopt a realistic grasp of relationship purposes and instil a sense of equality, fairness, and teamwork along with lower expectations. This environment is called 'relationship framework' with objectives noted in the previous chapter. Thus, let us discuss its role and components in this chapter. The goal is to harmonize partners' grasps of their roles and duties for making their relationship successful or at least minimizing its potential setbacks.

The Primary Structure

'Relationship Framework' is just a setting for couples to relate civilly, communicate effectively, and reduce their relationship frictions. The best way to explain this framework is to identify and review its components, as laid out below in Table 6.1:

Table 6.1: Components of a Relationship Framework

	Details in
1. Relationships Root: **R-entity**	(Chapter Six)
2. Partners' commitment to teamwork	(Chapter Five)
3. Relationship expectations	(Chapter Three)
4. Relationship needs (success factors)	(Chapter Four)
5. Relationship principles—GARP	(Chapter Seven)
6. Relationship models	(Chapter Eight)

Components 2, 3, and 4 were discussed in Part I. R-entity will be elaborated further later in this chapter, while components 5 and 6 are discussed in detail in Chapters Seven and Eight. Still, to draw a total picture about their connections these six components are explained below briefly as well.

1. Relationships Root: R-entity

Relationships Root (or R-entity for simplicity) highlights the fact that relationships must be viewed as an independent entity separate from partners' needs and identities. R-entity is merely a concept to remind couples that *relationship needs are unique and not derivatives of their personal needs*. R-entity is also the glue that keeps all components of the relationship framework together. Another way to view R-entity is to consider it both the conscious and conscience of relationships, which couples always try to remember and apply when judging themselves, their partners, and their relationships. Therefore, R-entity acts like a virtual, fair referee in the minds of two trained partners, and thus minimizing their needs for marriage counsellors or mediators to resolve their conflicts. Together with the other elements of the relationship framework, it forces partners to stay *relatively* objective and endure much less frictions.

R-entity can be further viewed as an active third party (the third leg of a tripod) in relationships to keep partners as alert, stable, and objective as possible. Without this third leg, the other two (i.e., partners) cannot bear relationships' pressures. Building this type of mentality is hard, considering our passive, stubborn personalities. Grasping and practising this mentality in real life sound too illusory and theoretical. However, enough suggestions are included in this book to get an overall feel for R-entity and become a sensible judge of our relationships. Anyhow, the goal is to introduce this type of mentality into relationships and society slowly during the next few decades.

Some more details about R-entity are provided at the end of this chapter due to its importance for relationships.

2. Partners' Commitment to Teamwork

As stressed all along, mostly Chapter Five, a crucial task of a relationship framework is to **enforce** teamwork in marriages. Yet, without both partners' full commitment to teamwork, the objectives of the relationship framework cannot materialize. If partners' Egos and impatience defy teamwork, relationships' unique needs remain unfulfilled and their relationship would be in jeopardy. Relationship needs are discussed below and in Chapters Four and Eight.

3. Relationship Expectations

Valid and unrealistic expectations in modern relationships are suggested in Tables 4.1 and 4.2 respectively on page 65 in line with our convoluted modern mindsets, lifestyles, and culture. Nonetheless, the viability of relationship expectations change regularly and couples should grasp the implications of both valid and unrealistic expectations presented in Tables 4.1 and 4.2. Scholars should also monitor social changes regularly and offer logical changes in relationship expectations in line with people's personal needs in every few generations or so.

As mentioned in Chapter Four, the unrealistic expectations in Table 4.2 might also materialize automatically in successful relationships between mature partners. Yet, they must be seen only as fringe benefits of that particular relationship. The point is that couples must not start a marriage based on unrealistic expectations, which hardly materialize and last in relationships. It does not mean that their relationship is abnormal when they face the reality. Actually, fulfilling the expectations in Table 4.1 is a big success by itself. With this mindset, partners would not blame each other for unfulfilled expectations or fuss too much about them. Instead, couples must beware of both valid and unrealistic relationship expectations and adapt themselves to this setting by choosing a relationship model somewhat practical for their main personal needs, especially their desired levels of independence and dependence.

4. Relationship Needs

Relationship needs correspond with the realistic relationship expectations listed in Table 4.1. Fulfilling these needs boosts relationships' synergy. As outlined in Table 4.3, relationship needs also represent 'Couples Responsibilities' and 'Success Factors.' Still, this list is not an ultimate or comprehensive list. A complete list of relationship needs (success factors) should be developed soon after deeper analyses and contributions of scholars. Anyway, the more relationship needs are fulfilled, the more successful a relationship would be in the long run.

A more complete list of relationship needs (success factors) should be developed after deeper analyses and contributions of scholars. However, in this book, the objective is to go one step further and identify the main parameters for measuring the health of relationships objectively. These basic parameters (success factors) would be applicable to most relationships in the new era. This can be achieved by developing a relationship framework that can help couples monitor their relationships' health regularly and realistically. The framework would help them watch their grasp and handling of the relationship needs. Thus, they would no longer guess the purpose or the health of their relationships arbitrarily merely based on partners' sloppy interpretations. Instead of guessing (and constantly increasing) their level of expectations from relationships, couples learn to tame their perceptions about relationships' purposes. They try to focus only on those limited factors that are important and practical for the success of relationships. At least partners should know that expectations beyond certain limits are bound to cause relationship conflicts and breakdowns. They should know that pressing their personal needs over relationship needs would be a recipe for the collapse of their relationship. Therefore, they are aware of the risks they are taking if they insist on following their personal whims instead of staying within the boundaries of the relationship framework.

5. Relationship Principles—GARP

We can no longer depend on a natural course in relationships and then suddenly get serious and react when problems are out of control and partners feel defeated. A few decades ago, this reactive strategy might have worked and been justifiable when the potential for, and the types of, relationship problems were limited. Nowadays, however, with the overwhelming variety of relationship conflicts, a proactive approach is needed. We now need to anticipate and prevent relationship conflicts as much as possible. The new approach should be a preventative one. It must emphasize on educating couples in advance about relationship needs and principles. They should then be taught to monitor their relationships continuously for signs of trouble.

In addition, couples should be trained to perceive (and expect) separation as a most likely outcome of relationships in the new era, anyway.

Accordingly, couples need a list of practical principles that can guide their mindsets and behaviour in their relationships. These guidelines draw certain boundaries that experts agree on as a viable mechanism for keeping relationships healthy. They should be studied and revised according to social values and changes regularly. These Generally Acceptable Relationship Principles (GARP) are discussed in detail in the next chapter.

6. Relationship Models

We simply cannot invent a certain relationship model to fit all couples or infinite varieties of models to suit the infinite types of couples' personalities. Therefore, it makes sense to identify a few models that can accommodate most people who believe in R-entity. Every model offers a particular setting for partners to relate and communicate according to their lifestyle priorities and capacities to exchange passion and compassion naturally. Relationship models are discussed in Chapter Nine.

Having a handful relationship models to choose from gives partners a chance to be specific about the kind of lifestyle they wish to share with each other based on their personalities and needs. A particular model feels most sensible to each couple base on partners' personal needs and how they expect to share or bear them. Still, every model offers an effective process of relating in relationships as long as couples can envision and accept the roles they should play to succeed. By choosing a particular model, couples learn to curb their wild perceptions about the potentials and purposes of relationships. They stop seeking an ideal relationship or criticizing the limited features of some relationship models. As explained in Chapter Nine, couples are goaded to initially choose the Relationship Model that emphasizes on partners' independence and then move up to the higher level models as (and if) their relationship matures and their experiences allow the progress, while they keep their personal needs in mind.

The above six components of the relationship framework must work together to create a productive relationships environment and help partners relate actively.

More Details about R-entity (Relationships Root)

To better grasp R-entity, let us view it from a different angle as well: In business partnerships, we identify the goal of the business and develop strategies for prospering it separate from its owners' identities. Obviously, business partners contribute to, and benefit from, the outcome of the operation. However, the vision and tools for running the business, the strategies to make it flourish, and the means of measuring its performance are all separate from partners' personalities or needs. Partners' personalities and management styles affect the success of their business. Yet, we do not define the goals and requirements of a business as the sum of the personal needs (or objectives) of its owners. For a successful business, it should be viewed as an independent entity with specific needs and goals of its own. Usually partners take special courses to raise their managerial skills and learn about planning and performing organizational and business duties. They do not change their personalities because they must run a business, but mainly learn about the requirements of running a business by viewing it as a dynamic entity enriching partners' lives only if it prospers and stays healthy itself. They adjust themselves to the requirements of their business, not the other way around like the customary practice in marriages. Even for a simple business operation, nowadays, partners must learn a lot about planning, budgeting, marketing, negotiating, accounting, performance measurement, decision-making process, etc. This is the type of mentality and strategy that spouses need as well. Managing 'relationships' has equal, if not more, demands and importance, after all.

Thus, marriage should be treated as carefully and viewed as an independent entity, too. Relationship expectations were not as complex and demanding even a few decades ago. Thus, developing a new vision and approach to run this important partnership effectively is imperative. A marital partnership is many folds more complex and demanding than any business partnership, because the cost of failure is much higher. The emotional aspect of such failure is horrendous and financial aspects might prove substantial in most cases. Thus, it must be viewed with as much focus and independence as any business venture is viewed. R-entity simply provides the opportunity of bringing a similar level of discipline to the concept we call *relationships*. The objective is to specify its unique needs and operational mechanisms independent from the personal needs of partners. Nowadays, relationships are starting to resemble a business and too calculating, anyway. Most partners seek more things and wealth from their relationships, and they ensure these assets are properly identified and registered for a likely separation. Meanwhile, they ask for unlimited compassion (and ELove), too, which usually comes across as hypocritical.

Someone might claim that the emotional aspects of marital relationships make them different from business partnerships. However, the fact that 'relationships' are more emotional than business indeed imposes even more need for caution and care. Relationships now require even a more stringent process and mechanism to ensure its success amidst all other personal and social pressures, both structural and emotional ones. Viewing 'relationships' as independent entities would not undermine their emotional value. In fact, it would generate better ideas and more time for compassion once the unreasonable needs and expectations of partners are eliminated. The growing high emotional aspect of relationships indeed exerts a bigger need for effective communication schemes than it is necessary for organizations. Thus, couples should stop taking relationships for granted, or ignore the need for special education and high awareness to master it. Rather, they must start viewing it as a separate entity (R-entity) from day one and focus on its unique needs more tenderly and clearly, instead of only pampering their own personal needs and Egos.

By the way, while R-entity feels like an abstract, dreary concept to grasp and follow, it can be mixed with the concept of MLove, which is explained in this and other books by this author, to create a meaningful, productive, and smooth process for enriching our relationships.

At the same time, it seems quite plausible that the concept of R-entity was already understood intuitively and practised rather naturally in the older cultures. It is just modern societies that have now become so irresponsible and spoiled.

Once the concept of R-entity finds universal appreciation, it will serve couples immensely. It will prevent partners from focusing on their personal needs selfishly, or even each other's needs, at the cost of ignoring the reality of relationships these days. Instead, couples would think mostly about the welfare of *relationships* as a third vital entity (R-entity) that imposes a set of specific, modest requirements for achieving certain goals. Accordingly, the society will begin to adopt suitable values, while promoting the unique needs of relationships as well. For example, societies can begin discouraging too many hours of work out of greed or superficialities. Family values could find a new perspective. Overall, R-entity says to each partner:

> "I don't care what your personal needs are. And you can keep fulfilling your needs or your partner's as effectively as you can. But remember that you should entertain and nurture me regularly, if you're interested in keeping me alive and active. I want good nutrition and your utmost awareness about my needs. If your Egos, idiosyncrasies, or learning disabilities prevent you from understanding my needs and rules, then just don't even bother coming

close to me. I know I sound arrogant expecting you put my needs ahead of yours or your partner's needs, but that is the only way I can stop you two from getting on each other's nerves and destroying me in the process, too."

With less (expectations), partners contribute more towards their relationship's health and integrity. This basic approach stops partners from imposing their idiotic, erratic expectations on relationships. Instead, they recognize their roles in keeping R-entity alive, while boosting their independence and dignity, too. Nowadays, we are merely suffocating R-entity with our never-ending personal expectations and needs.

Surely, every relationship has some unique characteristics based on personal preferences and intelligence of its partners. However, its general format and properties should always fall within R-entity's modest guidelines. This is the same principle that governs in business, too. The general needs and processes of business are not dependent upon the type of business or its owners' personalities. Some businesses are complex and huge, and some are small. Yet, the general business guidelines apply to all types of businesses all over the world. In relationships, then, each partner should honour those primary rules that are necessary for being in a relationship. These rules have nothing to do with partners' needs and dreams about the meaning and purposes of relationships. In fact, partners' specific needs and preferences related to relationships should not be in conflict with the requirements of R-entity. Rather, their needs should make sense within the context of R-entity. This is true, since R-entity advocates partners' independence and individuality. All the logical needs of partners are supported by R-entity. Therefore, when partners' personal needs contradict R-entity, it mostly reflects the irrationality of their needs. They might be too artificial or fantastical.

Of course, the success of a relationship requires partners' abilities to grasp and observe R-entity. In some situations, one or both partners might get bored. Or they get fed up with the efforts required to sustain a healthy R-entity. Some people are simply not made to be in relationships, the same way that not everybody has the right temperament to be an entrepreneur. Partners may feel they are sacrificing too much (by repressing their personal needs) in order to feed R-entity. For example, their excessive need for ELove is left mostly unfulfilled within a relationship framework driven by the concept of R-entity. In those cases, when facing a needy partner, R-entity advocates that separation might be a better option than hurting each other forever by more demands and nagging.

Obviously, two needy people can always choose to start (or continue) a relationship filled with their exaggerated needs and expectations. As long as they really know the risks of doing it outside the norms supported by R-entity, they are welcome to take their chance. They may even succeed in their adventurous journey. Nonetheless, those exceptions are based on partners' freewill and hopefully their full awareness of the associated risks. Knowing the risks of starting a relationship outside the R-entity boundaries might actually keep them conscious and proactive enough about their relationship to make a success out of it, despite the odds.

We assume we understand our personal needs and we find them quite justified, too. However, how authentic and useful they really are, and how they can satisfy us in the long run, is doubtful. Insisting on, or resisting, our needs and temptations is a personal decision, though. The trick is to test the sensibility of our needs in the context of R-entity when we want to be in a relationship. And for this, we should define the requirements of R-entity and develop a mechanism to measure the personal needs of partners against them. The big question is no longer if partners are compatible enough based on some criteria. Rather, the question is whether partners are equipped (mentally and emotionally) to be in an R-entity driven relationship.

Chapter Seven

Relationship Principles

Some tribal, religious, or cultural *principles* used to help humans manage their relationships until recently. Those ethics and etiquettes, ordinarily informal but clear, guided couples to live in some form of harmony. Surely, those outmoded family structures are no longer applicable or useful in new societies. Yet, the question is whether people can coexist peacefully without some sensible principles and laws to keep families in a relatively coherent harmony in the new world. The answer in the author's opinion is a resounding NO. Thus, the objective of this book has been to develop a mechanism for returning order and harmony to relationships, despite the gloomy prospect.

Starting perhaps only half a century ago, suddenly the old relationship principles have eroded along with the advent of so-called progressive societies and mentalities. Those sacred principles have become obsolete considering the emergence of new lifestyles, women's new role in society and organizations, and other symptoms of human struggle to prove his/her spirit and individualism. Personalities have changed and people have become more complex without any expertise to deal with one another effectively. Individuals' needs have skyrocketed and their expectations from relationships and life have increased, yet their patience and morality have declined drastically. The modern society has just propagated arrogance, extravagance, sexuality, crude life philosophies and mottos, and unlimited artificial needs.

Now we stand at the junction of history, quite incapable of relating to one another emotionally, effectively, and efficiently. Thus, we suffer due to our substandard relationships and our anguish heightens daily, simply because we ignore the current cultural deficiencies. We are unaware of the risks that the lack of relationship principles has caused. The excruciating hurdles of relationships, mainly due to rising personal idiosyncrasies, are affecting us directly and fiercely, while social complexities increase as well. Human interactions, at work, at home, and in society have become less sincere and manageable all around. Family relationships, in particular, have suffered in terms of couples' aptitude for sincerity, communication, and parenting. Instead, partners' oversensitivity and dogmatism are lowering the longevity of relationships. In all, no Generally Acceptable Relationship Principles (GARP) exist to guide couples or help them relate in their relationships.

Certainly, relationship problems and their sources are quite complex, yet mostly relate to the absence of GARP to help us grasp and respect each other's boundaries according to new social values. A point emphasized in this book is that humans' innate shortfalls, mainly Ego, hinder their abilities to relate to one another without authoritative guidelines, because they lack enough objectivity to run their relationships naturally. GARP can fill this gap and gradually turn into some viable, truthful social norm. It can minimize power struggles (domination of one partner or gender) and can help couples relate effectively. It should be developed gradually and updated regularly in line with social changes and research to, i) reflect human nature and needs, and ii) offer practical guidelines for a harmonious companionship.

GARP can be developed mainly based on the relationship needs listed at the end of Chapter Four. Accordingly, a replica of GARP is offered at the end of this chapter in Appendix 7-A. It provides a general idea to readers and a ground for further expansion by scholars.

The bottomline is that we must be willing to sacrifice in some respects to gain the peace of manageable relationships. And we must learn to tame our Egos in order to accept and honour GARP. The wedding woes we exchange superficially must be strengthened by GARP. In a sense, GARP is a refined set of etiquettes to help couples get along in their relationships. As demonstrated in Appendix 7-A, GARP merely provides all the points raised in this book about Relationship Framework in a simple narrative format.

The following questions need some elaboration, though, thus tackled in the remainder of this chapter in order to boost the readers' convictions to propagate GARP:

A. Can GARP really solve our relationship problems?
B. Is developing GARP feasible?
C. How can GARP be developed and propagated?
D. What a replica of GARP looks like?

A. Can GARP Solve Our Relationship Problems?

Yes, it can, in at least two ways: i) By providing a direction for relationships, and ii) by raising partners' objectivity. It would also fulfil a dozen objectives listed below once it is developed professionally with good details and instructions.

List of GARP's Objectives

1. *GARP can help us* **capture and propagate the features of a successful relationship.** It will provide the list of success factors in relationships, like the ones offered in Chapter Three. It will show how a relationship thrives, what it achieves, and what we can expect from it. Thus, GARP replaces the arbitrary (subjective) rules and criteria that couples currently

use for running their relationships or assessing its viability. GARP will bring objectivity back into relationships.

2. *GARP can help us* **realize our psychological limitations as human beings.** It can show how our personal quirks cause relationship chaos. GARP can enhance partners' sensitivities towards each other's needs, harmonize their expectations from their relationship, and give them a practical outlook about the substandard setting of relationships.
3. *GARP can help us* **realize why individuals' psychological defects are not easily repairable.** It will emphasize on finding the means of circumventing and bearing people's defects as much as possible, instead of nagging or criticizing them. Some of the ideas discussed in this book about human psychology can be adopted as *principles* and included in GARP. For example, we can agree that, as a valid principle, 'People can hardly change themselves.' One reason is that for changing oneself requires access to the depth of one's unconscious to change one's cognition. He/she must draw upon some extraordinary energy and spirituality to become a better human. A principle in GARP might reflect that 'The prevalent positive thinking mottos that claim people change themselves by will and boost their lives can hardly provide the profound conviction and guidelines required for deep mental adjustments through meditation and self-awareness.
4. *GARP can help us* **realize that the majority of people now perceive personal independence as their highest social value.** Thus, new relationship models and principles should stress on this primary fact: that couple's need and demand for individualism and independence cannot be restricted in relationships. This is a modern perspective after the advent of the women's lib movement and race equality struggles. Despite the common logical goal of seeking dependence in relationships, which is also in line with humans' instinctual need for it, our desire for independence is overwhelming every thought and action we engage in, nowadays. Thus,

GARP must support this general trend that is preoccupying people. Then, for pursuing this basic principle consistently, a high demand is on people to plan their personal lives rather independently, too, while keeping their expectations from relationships low accordingly. This means maintaining their financial independence, too, while respecting the spirit of cooperation and teamwork in marriages more than ever.

5. *GARP can help us* **realize that a doomed relationship should be ended civilly and easily.** To insist on correcting the inherent personality flaws of our partners, or retaliating relentlessly to make them suffer, is futile and childish. Once we believe in GARP's objectives and other facts discussed throughout this book, we realize our partners' helplessness in terms of their personality flaws and perceptions. With this mindset, we might at last see the futility of our lifelong struggle to either change our partners to suit our needs, or retaliate in order to hurt them the way they hurt us. Partners might find GARP, and the idea of stirring objectivity into relationships, beyond their patience or capacity. In that case, submitting to a friendly separation is their smartest option. Ending unmanageable relationships should be a natural and automatic process.
6. *GARP can help us* **recognize that the focus for correcting relationship conflicts is not our partner, but ourselves.** As reiterated often in this book, the only way for managing relationships is by having each partner work on his/her own flaws individually and honestly forever. They must commit themselves to become a better person regardless of its likely benefits for their relationship. A partner's decision to be a better person and means of pursuing this arduous mission is a personal matter and challenge. Partners should not press each other in hopes of creating better persons or saving their marriage. It does not work this way. Changing one's attitude is a personal challenge and needs conviction, which cannot be forced on someone. A decision to change lies only in the

hands of each partner. Thus, our demands and retaliations only make the matter worse.

The goal of self-awareness is to prepare a partner to curb his/her Ego, bear relationship flaws better, and accept his/her partner's shortfalls easier, unless the situation keeps deteriorating beyond tolerance.

7. *GARP can help us* **make our marital decisions, especially for starting or ending them, without the need to rely on official or religious formalities.** The more comprehensive and popular GARP becomes, the less supervision and rules people would need. Instead, GARP can help couples discuss their relationship issues objectively and judge the rationality of starting or ending them.

   Marriages begin on goodwill and optimism, yet we might get tired of our partner and wish to leave him/her, which is usually a natural sentiment that must be honoured. Then again, the main causes of separations, nowadays, are related to partners' juvenile rivalries and frictions, plus the absence of principles to guide couples and to measure their relationships' health regularly. If GARP can fill this gap, we would have much less need for bureaucratic, costly, and long processes to resolve our relationship conflicts.

8. *GARP can help us* **establish relationship norms that fit the socioeconomic profile of the current era.** It must also remain dynamic and be modified as humanity advances into more complex settings. All the evidences indicate that life and lifestyles will get painfully complex for many reasons. This is inevitable even if we adopt an optimistic viewpoint and imagine that we would not destroy humanity and the Earth altogether within a few centuries, or even decades perhaps. Nonetheless, GARP should fit the requirements of the time to remain effective. For example, partners' need for independence is the theme of the present era. In just a few decades, we, especially women, have become keen about individualism, which is now incorporated within all facets

of social life, including relationships. Many other structural and psychological changes have happened, including our rising appetite for sexuality, compassion, consumption, and children's prominent role and demands in family life. They all affect GARP's format, but nothing overwhelms GARP's theme in the 21st century as much as partners' raw, demands for identity and independence do. Of course, nobody can predict if people will not feel the opposite in a century or so, i.e., demand dependence more heroically. We might finally realize that marital compassion needs some principles of dependence. Then, swiftly, dependence might become the new fad and reality as much as independence is nowadays. This would actually be a rational progression that the author believes will happen. It will reflect either the humans' final defeat and desperation for peace, or their higher maturity, which is a possibility, although so remote.

As discussed before, couples are still not quite aware of the conflicts that their prominent demands for individualism have caused. They are unaware of the scope of confusions that their demands for large levels of both independence and dependence have created in their relationships. They subtly expect relationships to satisfy their needs for dependency, while they pretend and shout independence publicly. The subtle urge for dependence, while insisting on independence explicitly and noisily, is a major hurdle in relationships in the new era. We all must realize that we cannot have it both ways; to eat our cake and have it, too.

9. *GARP can help us* **develop the guidelines for couple's teamwork.** GARP must be somewhat proactive in terms of suggesting the basic models and principles of teamwork and negotiating. Actually, GARP should be developed with the intention of enforcing teamwork. Couples need tools to help them deal with a large variety of conflicts in relationships. Instead of suggesting all kinds of untested models or ideas, however, GARP's initial guidelines should remain general

and flexible, while more precise ones are developed and tested gradually. At least a few decades will pass before a well-crafted set of guidelines, especially for teamwork, is developed by experts and made available to couples.

10. *GARP can help us* **choose the right relationship model and pinpoint the compatibility factors between couples in order to minimize mismatches.** Partners can choose the right relationship model for them based on their needs and personalities by using GARP's guidelines. These guidelines might also pinpoint the areas of potential conflicts between partners according to the relationship model chosen. Instead of looking for compatibility factors, as attempted presently, GARP might suggest only those principles that would help couples *relate* effectively within the context of their unique (but organized) relationship. Preventing mismatches and pinpointing the wide range and areas of potential conflicts is another objective of GARP. This is different from the task of finding compatible partners. The existing compatibility tests have proven rather inadequate for developing effective relationships so far, anyway.
11. *GARP can help us* **work within a uniform framework to assess our relationships and communicate objectively.** Psychologists and marriage counsellors can communicate amongst themselves according to these guidelines, instead of suggesting a variety of personal or unproven methods. The existing techniques are not focused enough for tackling the roots of relationship problems. Thus, another objective of GARP is to create a uniform framework and language for psychologists and counsellors. Uniformity would not only make the diagnosis and treatment of relationship conflicts easier and transferable amongst experts, but also reduce the level of confusion and frustration for couples when each expert suggests different solutions and none of them works, anyway. Couples are suffering in their relationships already and do not need any additional source of confusion. They

need a universally tested system to help them one way or another—in or out of their relationships.

12. *GARP can help us* **view *relationships* as an independent, unique entity (R-entity), which is larger than the sum of the two partners in it.** R-entity, as a fundamental principle by itself, has to be included in GARP. The idea is to boost objectivity in relationships, instead of relying on subjective and unrealistic impressions of couples to define and manage their relationships based on their personal needs and Egos. Various features of R-entity are listed in GARP for clarity and application. Yet, other principles listed in GARP would support R-entity, too. R-entity is the nucleus for developing the relationship framework and its components. It is just the conceptual platform for us to boost our relationships.

The main purpose of GARP is to establish a solid ground for couples to relate emotionally, effectively, and efficiently. It can help them curb their rampant presumptions about themselves, their partners, and relationship purposes. It can become a point of reference, a defendable social norm, to measure couples' expectations and attitude. It can pinpoint the causes of marital clashes and misperceptions. GARP will also contain all the information and guidelines for constructing and maintaining the 'relationship framework' within its six crucial components listed in Table 6.1, Page 95.

Once the public understand the merits of GARP's plausible objectives and immense benefits for their relationships, they would feel more willing to stick to those sensible norms and principles, too. GARP will be an easy-to-read document for the public. It will enumerate the facts and guidelines regarding relationships according to the social setting of the time. The author believes that people would eventually appreciate the validity and significance of GARP's objectives. Thus, they will find it in their interest to modify their mindsets in order to make their relationships manageable and live in some form of harmony. In all, GARP is intended to become a practical Bible for relationships and mitigate people's antagonism.

B. Is Developing GARP Feasible?

Yes, it is, despite people's major cynicism and resistance at the outset. Of course, developing new guidelines for relationships is a great challenge in terms of its mechanics. Getting experts' universal acceptance of its contents is also tough, while some objective, intelligent authorities should continue monitoring, adjusting, and promoting relationship principles in line with people's mental progress. Thus, the answer to the feasibility of developing GARP remains a reserved yes. The reservation is with respect to the timeframe required for most principles to be deemed 'acceptable' as social norms and included in GARP. The other reservation is the timeframe for most people to build the right mindset for adopting GARP.

However, creating a simple preliminary format for GARP is not an impossible task. It can be easily developed around the relationships' realistic needs (success factors) listed in Chapter Four. Let us assume that this is a realistic list, and in line with our social values at the present time. The list must be modified regularly, of course, to reflect social changes, while keeping the unrealistic expectations out. Every 'relationship need' listed in Chapter Four can be expanded into a few direct, practical principles, which can guide the task of fulfilling that particular need. The replica of GARP presented at the end of this chapter (Appendix 7-A) is created in this manner. That is, every need in Chapter Four is expanded into a bunch of principles in GARP. All we need for creating GARP is innovative ideas (like the radical solutions in Chapter Eleven and those offered throughout this book) to reassess relationships in the existing social environment, and then devise basic principles to fulfil the most urgent needs of relationships and couples. The large volume of hypotheses presented throughout this book can be verified and included in GARP gradually to boost couples' understanding of relationships, their hurdles, etc.

We need principles that raise teamwork to curtail the level of marital frictions. We know the basics already. Especially, individualism and independence have become the dominating themes of the new society. Therefore, we have the platform to build principles around these basic needs of individuals. We should identify a practical balance between couples' personal needs and the relationship needs in the new era and define those boundaries in GARP. Once we pinpoint the big conflicts between personal needs and the relationship needs, we should be able to devise effective principles and then learn to live with our choices in harmony.

Thus, in the author's opinion, creating GARP can begin as soon as society agrees that we need it. This book only hopes to spread the seeds for future thoughts, while growing people's interest to reassess and revamp their outmoded mentalities about relationships rather fast. After all, we are all seeking the same objective: to be happier in our relationships. Then again, when we check social realities and people's mentalities at this time, a full-fledged application of GARP may not become a universal concept until the 22nd century. The author is rather inclined to choose the year 2115 as a plausible timeframe for GARP being fully developed with a universal acceptance and taught at high schools. This arbitrary date might appear too optimistic or pessimistic depending on the views of various groups. The author realizes this fact, too, while hoping that a plan for developing GARP is devised as soon as possible.

C. How Can GARP Be Developed?

Despite its slow universal acceptance in the immediate future, GARP should be developed and expanded seriously based on trial and error and research findings. The success of GARP depends on our faiths about its ability to help relationships.

However, the author believes that this task would be somehow imposed upon us, whether we like it or not, sooner or later. We will be forced eventually to do something about the agony of relationships due to the lack of principles. We will soon get fed up with our arbitrary, raw assessments of relationships as well as our emotional decisions about the level of tolerance required in relationships. Maybe our children learn from our mistakes and shattered hopes to find a soul mate. It is merely a matter of time and the level of our tenacity to pursue idealism, instead of accepting the existing sad realities.

It helps if scholars and interested groups agree about the importance of GARP and get involved right away. The public should also recognize the benefits of GARP and ask for its development actively, while learning about its purposes and adjusting their mentalities. Once a good platform is defined and accepted by prominent sociologists, psychologists, and the population at large, modifying and expanding GARP would be an automatic process like most other social processes in progressive societies of the future. We merely have to remain optimistic and hope that future societies are given a chance to flourish out of the chaos we have caused for ourselves and our children. A non-profit foundation can ideally be created to oversee the development and dissemination of GARP.

In terms of propagating GARP, we must simply introduce it at as many public forums and social gatherings as possible. Experts must advocate this book's objectives. They must find innovative ways of informing the public about the flaws of our existing ways. They should do more empirical research and be more proactive in terms of changing couples' mindsets about relationships.

Despite the major initial resistance, GARP's advantages will become clear to the public soon when managing relationships gets totally out of control and couples' frustration cripples the society. Liberal and logical people begin to join in and adopt GARP in order to test new options for their relationships. They will support the rather radical ideas open-mindedly. The result will eventually goad sceptical people to join the movement, too, in order to mitigate their hardships and loneliness.

Books can also help mainly to comprehend our personality flaws in terms of dealing with others, especially our partners. They must show that animosity, arrogance, and retaliation are unproductive, because such attitude and approach only make it harder for people to perceive each other's intentions correctly and react to them calmly. We may also realize that as human beings eager to exploit our potentials fully, we are wasting too much time and energy on the petty problems of relationships. This is absurd and a sin.

Explaining the mechanisms of developing GARP in detail is beyond the scope of this book. Yet, the principles discussed throughout this book provide enough material to begin the process. Let us hope they will prove fruitful as steppingstones for further thoughts and discussions during the next hundred years. Let us join to do this urgent task. Meanwhile, a replica of GARP is presented in Appendix 7-A only as an example of ideas that could be included in GARP. It is not meant to be complete or correct. It is prepared mainly by expanding the relationship needs listed at the end of Chapter Four. It should be expanded eventually to include a large number of radical solutions like the ones proposed in Chapter Eleven as well as the ideas in the other parts of this book.

D. What a replica of GARP looks like?

See Appendix 7-A (a replica of GARP on page 122)

GARP's Main Challenge

On the one hand, developing GARP and a new mindset about relationships seems feasible and necessary, although it would take time and patience. In fact, GARP might be the only wise solution, in the author's opinion, to manage our relationships in a realistic manner and save our societies as well. The main challenge is to keep our faith in GARP as a viable solution for our relationship problems.

On the other hand, it might seem naïve to assume that companionship needs of individuals, such a complex subject it is, can be solved by any mechanism (e.g., GARP) quickly or at all. Those very same problems and hurdles that prevent us from finding a good companion or maintaining a relationship —as discussed throughout this book—would also affect the implementation of new mechanisms. Resistance to change will be a huge hurdle. Mostly our Egos and conditioned mentalities to perceive relationships only in certain ways will stop us from changing our attitudes. GARP must eventually sink into our cultures, so that we feel and handle it naturally.

Overcoming our old habits and urges to entertain GARP or other mechanisms will be difficult, although everybody should logically realize the benefits of adopting a fair, sensible GARP fast. Accountants have used Generally Accepted Accounting Principles (GAAP) to guide them in their financial dealing and wheeling. They are supposed to use GAAP for communicating among themselves efficiently and ethically. They have adopted GAAP and sworn to observe it. Yet, they often forget their commitment to GAAP when personal incentives supersede their sense of obligation to a higher cause. In our greed-ridden society, even the officials of certified banks and investment companies ignore their sacred obligations. People lose their life savings left and right. We have all kinds of traffic rules and guidelines developed for the safety of the public, but our Egos and tempers make us disregard those rules even at the expense of our own lives and the risk of severe punishments. These diseases have infected our relationships, too. In fact, in relationships, the complex emotional issues make it even more difficult to maintain a sense of commitment to GARP easily. Nonetheless, GAAP helps accountants a lot and our traffic laws bring major order to our lives, despite the drunken idiots who intentionally disobey the laws and kill people. Society is benefiting, nonetheless, from GAAP and traffic laws and all the other rules we enforce to align our thoughts and actions. It is time to benefit from GARP, too. Or, at least, we must begin to envision such a fruitful mechanism, so that people can benefit from its full potentials in a century or so.

GARP might appear doomed at the outset by its attempt to generalize ideas that touch individuals' emotions and urges. The idea of formulating some principles about relationships by pursuing logical analyses and reasoning sounds absurd and naïve already. GARP feels like a bizarre approach in a society where objectivity and logic seem to have lost their meanings. Clearly, both personal needs and relationship expectations are vastly deep-rooted and emotional. Their psychological effects and power are controlling our mindsets and faiths. Overall, relationships and couples' behaviour are too complex to study scientifically readily. Still, the notion of introducing GARP seems to be the only option left for society to mend the chaotic state of relationships. Of course, it is clear that applying rules to relationship issues, and human behaviour in general, has its limitations. Thus, the development of GARP will be gradual, partially based on trial and error. GARP must remain dynamic and progressive according to new findings and research.

Learning and Adjusting

The process of implementing GARP requires a lot of learning and adjusting. This is an immense responsibility that people and governments must assume collectively in a well-defined plan of action for social stability. The mission of convincing couples to replace their emotional decision processes with GARP would be difficult. They must accept the responsibility of observing their relationships' needs, despite their conflicting personal urges and Egos. They must demonstrate interest and a mental capacity to function within an objective framework.

This will take time and patience. Meanwhile, we should keep our faiths in GARP as a viable solution to our relationship problems. Actually, GARP might be the only solution, in the author's opinion, to manage our relationships better.

GARP can help us in many ways. It can help us recognize the causes of relationship problems. It can raise our awareness about our personal flaws and limitations gradually and we might learn how they affect our relationships. GARP can enhance our sensitivity towards our partners, instead of being oversensitive and demanding. It can help us appreciate that our partners' defects and limitations are crippling them; they are unaware of those flaws or unable to do something about them. GARP can prove useful for coping with our complex social settings. It can show how social changes are tainting our perceptions about everything, including our personal needs. It can identify the 'success factors' in relationships. At the very least, it can help us grasp the role we are expected to play even if we are unwilling or unable to adopt it due to our tenacities. Even this minimal awareness is useful. GARP might even mitigate the doomed prospect of humanity if it makes us mature and a bit more realistic about existence.

We humans have limited ability and patience to listen to, let alone learn about, any concept that threatens our crooked convictions and deep-rooted idiosyncrasies. Thus, believing in GARP would not be an easy task, never mind practising it. Yet, we must remain hopeful that some of us will benefit from GARP sooner or later. Despite all the foreseeable challenges, we need GARP badly and urgently.

GARP can possibly help a small group of people initially until it is propagated naturally in society after its benefits are proven. Two groups of people may never need or care about GARP. The first group consists of those lucky individuals who somehow find a good companion based on their simple lifestyles and managed expectations. We all envy those blessed couples. At the other extreme, some people are so defective psychologically that no rules or reasons can help them overcome their rampant urges and crooked personalities. Those falling between these two extremes —most of us—have manageable levels of psychological defects and destructive urges. This majority might eventually appreciate the potential of GARP, despite humans' instinctual resistance to change.

On the one hand, choosing GARP over our personal whims and ideals would be hard. Lowering our fanciful expectations from relationships would feel like an impossible mission.

On the other hand, it is rather easy and extremely useful to develop a set of simple principles for running our relationships more smoothly and effectively. It is especially crucial for giving youths a general guideline about the purposes, potentials, hassles, and most likely outcome of relationships in the new era.

Accordingly, the main purpose of this book is to stress on the need for changing our mentalities about relationships and seek the right criteria for their success. We might sense the benefits of this adjustment quickly, while the implementation of GARP will take many decades. Without our participation and dialogue, the sacred mission of implementing GARP will not get off the ground. We should believe in, and commit to, personal mental adjustment and begin acting now as well. The public and society should feel comfortable to adopt GARP and the 'relationship framework.'

Appendix 7-A

A Replica of GARP

The guidelines listed in GARP can be grouped and presented in a narrative format for the public's easy understanding. For this basic document, however, merely the relationship needs in Chapter 3 are organized in the following format:

Part I: Structure of GARP
Part II: Relationship Success Factors
Part III: Social Mechanisms Supporting GARP

Part I: Structure of GARP

The main structure of GARP is explained in this part:

P1. Partners see their relationship as an independent entity, which has specific needs and priorities. This concept is called R-entity for simplicity.

P1.1 Relationship needs are different from partners' needs.

P1.2 R-entity is not driven by partners' needs.

P1.3 Relationship needs supersede partners' needs.

P1.4 Relationship needs are developed and modified, as necessary, according to social settings and trends.

P1.5 Relationship needs are also dynamic based on fundamental changes in human nature over centuries.

P2. Spouses are independent financially and emotionally in principle, though they might agree on a more practical arrangement for them at the outset.

P2.1 Individualism and independence constitute the main social and relationship principles, nowadays, so they also dictate the foundation of 'relationship needs.'

P2.2 Individualism and independence dictate the rules and boundaries for partners to keep their expectations low and realistic within a suitable relationship model.

P2.3 Exceptions to the principle P2.2 are specifically noted in a contract between partners.

P3. Partners understand the Relationship Framework and its components in detail before entering a relationship.

P3.1 The 'Relationship Framework' offers a setting for couples to relate and communicate effectively.

P3.2 The Relationship Framework has 6 components:

- R-entity
- Partners' commitment to teamwork
- Relationship expectations
- Relationship needs (success factors)
- Relationship principles—GARP
- Relationship models

P3.3 The components of Relationship Framework are explained in Subsections… thru… (Page 95 in this book)

P4. Partners respect the Relationship Framework' rules.

P5. Partners' realistic relationship expectations are:

1. Sex
2. Communication
3. Compassion
4. Companionship
5. Teamwork
6. MLove
7. Friendship
8. Respect- Social acceptance
9. Personal Success
10. Financial stability

P6. Partners realize the risks of pushing the expectations in the table presented in Subsection P6.1.

P6.1 The unrealistic relationship expectations are:

1. Dependence
2. Security
3. SLove
4. ELove
5. Trust
6. Happiness
7. Commitment
8. Longevity

Part II: Relationship Success Factors

In this part, the characteristics of a successful relationship are outlined in line with the factors outlined in Table 4.3, Page 67.

A relationship would be successful if:

P7. Partners build and keep a basic level of emotional and intellectual connection, ideally with good chemistry.

P8. Partners relate actively and enjoy compatible lifestyles and preferences in line with their relationship model.

P9. Partners boost their self-awareness, communication, and Self, while reducing their Ego, Elove, and expectations.

P10. Partners realize the risks of their misperceptions about life and marital purposes damaging their marriages.

P11. Partners know everybody's personality is highly shaped and led by forces beyond his/her control. They realize how human nature's big flaws also infect marriages.

P12. Partners do not blame each other or whine constantly about their eccentricities.

P13. Partners know how to energize their communication.

P14. Partners enjoy having sex together along with adequate compassion.

14.1 Partners do not use sex as a tool for blackmailing, intimidating, or manipulating each other.

P15. Partners use mostly teamwork to run family affairs.

P16. Partners are compassionate and learn how to show it.

P17. Partners know the rules of friendship and stick to them.

P18. Partners do not try to change each other or push their mentalities on each other.

P19. Partners strive sincerely to develop trust between them, but do not make too much fuss about mistrust.

P20. Partners do not try to manipulate, control, or intimidate each other for any reason.

P21. Partners exchange respect and compassion, despite the difficulty of tolerating each other's idiosyncrasies.

P22. Partners are capable of promoting each other's needs for independence and dependence.

P23. Partners can support each other *somewhat* actively to pursue their personal goals and social ambitions.

P24. Partners are aware of the Ego, Model, and Self aspects of personality and their roles in their communications. They monitor the positive or negative impacts of these personality aspects on their lives.

P25. Partners know the meanings and workings of ELove, MLove, and SLove in their relationships.

P26. Partners have chosen the right relationship model that best fit their personalities and logical personal needs.

P27. Partners respect the boundaries set by their relationship model for managing their needs and expectations.

P28. Partners are familiar with, and actively advocate, GARP —as main principles of relationships. They use GARP, in particular, to stay objective in their relationship.

P29. Partners seek mediation and marital counselling when necessary, but only through GARP oriented experts.

P30. Partners strive to maintain their honesty and integrity.

P31. Partners are mentally trained to leave their relationship peacefully when reconciliation is not possible.

P32. Partners try to be tactful, mature, forgiving, patient and mentally stable.

P33. Partners do not adhere to spite, blackmail, or violence to convince each other or resolve their differences.

P34. Partners do not play games with each other.

P35. Partners do not depend on the government or religion to regulate their relationship.

P36. Partners have signed a contract at the outset to govern financial and other main aspects of their relationship, especially for the case of separation.

P37. Partners have compatible temperaments about finance and budgeting in line with a sensible plan for the long-term financial stability and welfare of the family.

P38. Partners envision the termination of relationships as a normal expectation in the new era.

P39. Partners believe that marital endings must be civil and quick.

P40. Partners gauge the state of their relationship regularly and discuss the contentious issues calmly.

Part III: Social Mechanisms Supporting GARP

In this part, the main mechanisms to promote GARP and the 'Relationship Framework' are listed:

P41. Social systems and mechanisms are modified in order to support and propagate GARP.

P42. Legal entities revamp their processes and laws in order to minimize their interference in relationships.

P42.1 The adjustments by the legal system and laws are for promoting individuals' independence.

P42.2 The legal system ensures that people realize that they are depending on themselves to protect their own rights in relationships rather than relying on the government to do it for them.

P43. Educational systems teach the relationship framework and its components to the public, especially to youths.

P43.1 Relationship principles, expectations, and needs should be taught at high schools as required courses.

P43.2 Relationship courses are treated most seriously. The passing grades for completing relationship courses at high schools are set extremely high and monitored by the Board of Education.

P43.3 Free counselling will be available to newlyweds to ensure they know the guidelines of the relationship framework and follow GARP to start their marriages. This would help them realize the nature and hurdles of relationships in the new era and enhance the chance for their marital longevity.

PART III

Relationship Models

And
Radical Solutions

Chapter Eight

How to Relate

The whole idea behind relationship models is to maximize couples' capacity and opportunity to relate as productively as possible in their marriages. In fact, many methods and models of *relating* exist that can help couples achieve this sacred goal. We need these models (as suggested later in this Chapter) to overcome so much marital conflicts, nowadays, which reduce couples' chances for building effective families and relating in meaningful ways.

Naturally, a special kind of 'relating'—usually bizarre—erupts in every relationship in line with partners' personalities, needs, and the peculiar relationship environment that grows without partners' conscious and ability to control. Couples try not to look careless or aloof, while hoping to develop some kind of civilized manner of relating gradually. They strive to keep their relationships under control according to the peculiar attributes of the relationship environment they have cultivated or emerged out of necessity. All along, most couples miss their chances to build good rapport and communication to avoid estrangement and hostility.

Thus, in the end, most couples seem mostly engaged in some kind of a game or retaliation, or behave passively around each other, to make the best of their marriages, while feeling trapped in a frustrating setting. Often a passive approach feels like the best strategy to minimize their quarrels and anxiety. Overall, partners usually fail and suffer, despite their efforts to build a rather productive and active type of relationship.

Accordingly, it seems that exploring and developing better means of relating and specifying a handful relationship models can help people and society a lot. After millenniums of trials and errors, it seems odd that we have not even considered the need for relationship models to help people relate or at least avoid getting into relationships with great potential for failure.

As a start, we can classify *relating* into 'active' versus 'passive.' A couple relates actively (or positively) when they can maintain positive Emotions, Effectiveness, and Efficiency. The three Es are active. This ideal happens when partners are committed to teamwork and have chosen a relationship model that best fits their personal needs and personalities. They know how to live within the parameters of the model, too. On the other hand, sometimes, partners have already given up on the idea of enjoying an ideal relationship together. Therefore, they somehow learn to relate passively, instead of separating. The passive way means minimum expectations from relationship, yet keeping it manageable. In this case, one or more of the three Es are compromised—partners are passive regarding the welfare of their relationship, yet do their best to keep it going smoothly. Anyway, both types of relationships are acceptable as long as couples are able to observe the realistic relationship expectations listed in Table 4.1. Actually, most relationships, nowadays, are based on a form of *passive relating,* although partners are not quite conscious about their method of relating.

It is important for partners to know about the way they are 'relating,' if at all, and acknowledge it, too. Next, they must find the means of facilitating their communications to increase the effectiveness of their relationship for that type of relating, i.e., active versus passive relating. Some couples keep getting a lot from their relationships, even though 'passive relating' is not an ideal condition. Recognizing and agreeing on the best option for them enhances their awareness to implement its particular needs effectively. Of course, if one partner insists on relating actively when the other is happy with passive relating, their relationship gets into trouble. If partners have different views about their relationship, no special model or mechanism is in place and their relationship rolls on an alienation course. Confusing messages between partners grow and frustrate them on a painful alienation course. Marriage counsellors can assist couples pursue a particular option (relationship model) and grasp its needs, implications, and outcomes.

How partners relate is a complex process requiring a full book of analyses. Obviously, the more the relationship needs listed in Chapter Four are satisfied, the higher would be the chances of couples *relating* to each other actively. And the higher the relationship model (partners' dependency level), the more actively they would be relating.

Of course, relating and communicating are two different concepts. In some instances, partners might enjoy a rather good communication between them, but still cannot relate, because they have different mentalities and lifestyle preferences. And sometimes they can relate, but lack adequate communication skills (or patience) to express themselves. Both cases cause problems. However, 'relating' is often a more vital factor for the success of relationships than 'communication.' The reason is that at least partners agree on the relationship model they have chosen and remain truthful to its needs. The main factors for *relating* are partners' harmony in terms of philosophies, lifestyle preferences, priorities, and intelligence. Another vital factor is the role of their personality aspects (mostly modesty) in their daily lives and interactions, without Ego playing a big role. Higher modesty makes relating a lot easier. A reasonable level of flexibility and patience can also help partners express themselves better and relate more actively, too.

The passive and active modes of 'relating,' can be analysed around the three Es (emotions, effectiveness, and efficiency):

- **In terms of emotions**, partners' objective is to either enjoy each other's companionship (active relating), or bear each other without causing undue emotional distress or setback for each other (passive relating). While positive emotions reflect a high degree of love and connectedness, passive emotions reflect partners' appreciation of each other, care, and compassion. Knowing about humans' limitations and our partners' helplessness to change their attitudes enough for our liking enables couples to relate, even though it might not be as active emotionally as they would like it to be.
- **In terms of effectiveness**, partners' objective is to share ideas and agree on the means of pursuing their personal and common goals, instead of rivalry or sabotaging each other. They do this for both 'active' and 'passive' relating, but at different degrees. When they are eagerly supporting each other to achieve their personal objectives, they are active. However, when one or both partners are not showing enough interest in each other's affairs, they still could have a good relationship, passively. Then again, the urge to sabotage or retaliate is common in relationships where partners humiliate each out of spite or to prove their superiority. Generally, partners can relate effectively when they work together to establish the *right things* for their relationship and personal lives overall (active relating). In 'passive' relating, they just do not work enough together to increase the effectiveness of their relationship, but they also do not sabotage each other or show rivalry.
- **In terms of efficiency**, partners set their goals properly and economically for achieving productive results and satisfying their personal and common goals. Partners relate efficiently when they can work together to do *things right* rather than wasting each other's time and energy. They avoid wasting the emotional and financial resources that support R-entity.

Teamwork's importance for peace and civility in both active and passive relationship models can never be overestimated.

Some level of compatibility can always help couples fulfil the relationship needs listed in Chapter Four better and also relate rather actively. Partners should know both their compatibility and incompatibility factors that either boost or hinder their relationships. They must also know the methods of measuring their partners' compatibility for relating in the new era. Those compatibility factors must also demonstrate how successfully a couple is (or could be) 'relating' in an existing or planned relationship. Finally, they should measure partners' emotional capacities and connection, which are also vital for raising their relationship's effectiveness and efficiency. The score would show the degree of partners' passive or active relating and the suitability of the relationship model they have adopted.

Relationship Models' Features

Ideally, relationship models should be developed around the following four main criteria:

1. Partners' capacity and efforts to relate *actively*,
2. Degree and order of *Relationship Needs* satisfied,
3. The level of *dependency* partners wish (or are able) to build,
4. The proximity of *partners' personal needs*.

An elaborate 'factor analysis' could consolidate the above four criteria (factors) and provide a fine scientific Relationship Needs ranking. However, a simple 'relationship needs tree' is needed now for the purpose of this book. One way to go about it is to develop a subjective list of ranked success factors for present societies. This satisfies the criterion # 2 on the above list the most. For example, discussions in this book indicate that partners' knowledge and application of the relationship framework, commitment to certain relationship principles, and teamwork, etc. should get the highest rankings on this list.

Another approach is to develop a 'relationship needs tree' according to the dependency capacity (maturity) of partners. That is, as partners depend more on each other for support and love, their relationship rating advances. This satisfies a good mix of the criteria 2 and 3 on the above list the most. Surely, the more partners wish to depend on each other (# 3), the more complex (but also more complete) their relationship becomes and the more of relationship needs (# 2) are fulfilled as well. How well each 'relationship need' is satisfied also affects their relationship's level of completeness (success). Thus, partners' 'dependence' level signifies the relationship needs and model suitable for them. Let us review this primary approach before another criterion (# 4) is added to the final structure of this book's *Relationship Models*.

Relationship Needs Tree

The author believes that a dozen relationship models can be developed eventually to satisfy most personalities capable of building functional families. For simplicity in this book, let us identify five levels of partners' dependency in line with the particular relationship needs shown in Diagram 8.1.

Dependency Level (Relationship Model)	Order (Tree) (Relationship Level)
5 ↑	Selfless love (SLove)
4	Dependence/Personal Success
3	Friendship/Egoistic love (ELove)
2	Compassion/Model love (MLove)
1	Co-existence

Diagram 8.1: Relationship Needs Tree

The notations SLove, ELove, and MLove shown in the diagram were defined in Chapter Three, which indicate that the higher we climb up the tree, the more sincere and dependable couples' level of love would be.

The five relationship models and levels in Diagram 8.1 are explained in the next chapter. First, however, it is crucial to understand the relationship needs in diagram 8.1 in relation to the models specified. The relationship needs (success factors) were listed in Chapter 4. Ideally, couples must satisfy all those needs together as much as possible. Yet, couples must fulfil some of those needs with the higher urgency noted in Diagram 8. The tentative ranking in this diagram reflects the urgency and importance of certain factors for relationships' success as explained below:

1. The five 'dependency' rankings (levels) reflect the urgency and complexity of the relationship needs. The higher the ranking, the more **complex** relationship needs become.
2. Conversely, a lower ranking reflects the higher **urgency** of those preliminary relationship needs that partners should fulfil first without putting dependency pressures on their relationship, too, until they learn about each other and their unique relationship's needs, mature, and gradually become more dependent upon each other naturally—and surely not forcefully from day one.
3. The higher we go up the tree, the more dependent partners become on each other and the harder they should work to fulfil those needs.
4. On the other hand, a low dependency level shows partners' admirable capacity for independence, instead of burdening their relationship with their demands.
5. The above four points demonstrate that the more urgent a relationship need is, the harder each partner should work independently to make a success of their relationship and also fulfil his/her personal needs.
6. Partners must understand and fulfil the less complex needs of relationships first, which are also more urgent, before advancing to higher dependency levels. The problem in relationships, nowadays, is that couples do the opposite. That is, they naively believe that they can easily start their

relationships at the highest dependency level and impose all their complex needs, including ELove and SLove, upon each other right away.

7. The higher we move up on the above tree, the more solid a relationship gets, because more relationship expectations are satisfied naturally after partners learn about each other, gain more patience to handle their conflicts, and grasp the relationship needs and framework.
8. At the upper relationship levels, even the rather unrealistic expectations (listed in Table 4.2), including selfless love, are satisfied.
9. The higher partners move up the tree, the more they are expected to have balanced their needs for dependence and independence personally and in terms of relating to one another.
10. As a whole, in the lower levels of the tree, partners stress on their independence. They move up the hierarchy only when they can prove their genuine interest and maturity to respond to each other's dependency needs as well (on top of their independency) in a proper manner.

An ironic conclusion from the Relationship Needs Tree is that partners need a high degree of maturity to gain even the capacity for grasping the meaning and means of depending on each other. Initially, this conclusion seems rather contrary to the general belief that we need more maturity for becoming an independent person. However, there is no contradiction here if we think about the matter deeply. Of course, a high degree of maturity and enlightenment is required to achieve personal independence. Yet, at the same time, we need even a higher level of maturity and enlightenment to become selfless enough to accept some sort of mutual dependency to others and allow others to depend on us, too.

This is an important point to ponder for understanding our independency needs and gauging our maturity level. Lots of courage and wisdom is required to ask for, or allow, higher dependencies in our lives, and also satisfy the obligations that go with it in the right way. This is a major fact (and hurdle) in relationships, which is lost to couples with the least amount of maturity and wisdom, yet demanding lots of dependency quite selfishly without realizing or honouring their own obligations.

A major reason for so much conflict in relationships is that couples do not have a particular relationship model to guide them. Yet, most couples imagine they can start and maintain a relationship at the highest level of the relationship needs tree automatically and fulfil all its *complex* requirements *urgently*. It is clear by now how insensible this expectation is. Couples must realize that moving up the relationship needs takes time, patience, and devotion by showing their sincerity and security. It is like a case of friendship that grows gradually, naturally, and with minimal expectations slowly. Partners must be really mature in terms of personality, lifestyle, and priorities to reach a higher level in the relationship needs tree. This progression is not by partners' desire or choice, but rather automatic, as a natural outcome of partners' compatibility, personality, and needs. Thus, partners should be realistic about the relationship model they choose. They should not demand high dependency until they demonstrate their capacity to stay humble and free from Ego. Especially, newlyweds should choose the lowest relationship model at the beginning and hope to move upward based on their actual encounters, actions, and reactions over a long time, while facing personal and relationship conundrums as wisely and smoothly as possible. In reality, however, they do just the opposite. That is, they assume they are equipped to deal with each other's high dependency needs from the start. They also assume they have the right to expect such a thing—total devotion and dependency—rather naturally from their partners simply because they have just married.

Now, to strengthen relationship models' capacity further, we can add the requirements of criterion # 4 listed on page

133 and gauge the effect of bringing partners' personal needs into the design of Relationship Models' structure.

Personal Needs Tree

A set of growing innate needs like those shown in Diagram 8.2. drives humans. Basic needs, such as food and shelter, are at the bottom of this order (the needs tree). Social interaction and recognition are in the middle. The higher needs consist of self-esteem and actualization. According to this theory, people move up the needs tree as their lower needs are satisfied. For this book's purpose, only the personal needs related to couples' relationship interactions and conflicts are of interest.

5. Self-actualization/Spirituality
4. Status/Recognition
3. Social
2. Security
1. Shelter & Food

Diagram 8.2: Personal Needs Tree

Relationship Needs Forest!

Now, it is interesting and informative to study whether and how couples' personal needs (Diagram 8.2) coincide with their relationship needs (Diagram 8.1). Diagram 8.3 (in the next page) shows this comparison, with personal needs shown on the horizontal axis and relationship needs on the vertical axis. Five relationship models are defined in this diagram as well, in line with dependency criterion (# 4) used in Diagram 8.1.

The term 'Relationship Needs Forest' is used only for two reasons: First, to reflect the complexity of the relationship needs when only two trees (personal and relationship need trees) stand side by side and contradict one another too often. Second, to separate relationships' complex needs in Diagram 8.3 from the basic ones in Diagram 8.1. That is, the pressures of couples' personal needs make their relationship needs even more complicated than the case where partners are less needy and demanding from their relationship. After all, couples' raw personal needs obscure relationship needs very much and very quickly, beyond the preliminary needs of a simple and natural relationship. Nowadays, even the basic relationship needs have become too complex, like a dense forest, to grasp and satisfy.

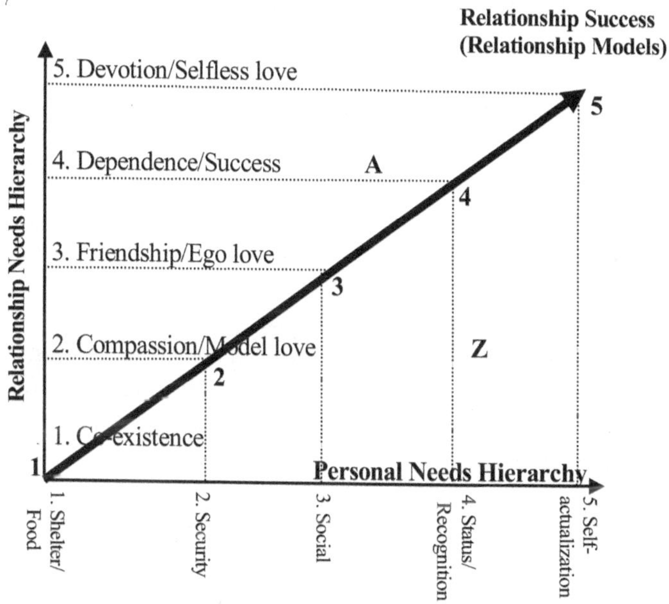

Diagram 8.3: Relationship Needs Forest

An interesting point about Diagram 8.3 is that the vertical axis, 'relationship needs,' is placed at the left of the horizontal axis (i.e., personal needs), where shelter and food are, which depicts 'relationship needs' as a general 'basic need' for us.

This makes sense, since companionship and compassion are crucial needs, nowadays, even for a starving, homeless person, although we usually view relationships as a social need.

Obviously, humans' need for a companion has found the highest value in modern societies. (This might sound like an odd statement considering the chaotic state of relationships in the new era. However, the fact that we have so much difficulty finding a companion is actually turning 'relationships' into a more scarce and urgent need.) Anyway, finding a companion is perceived by the majority of us as a basic need—at least in affluent countries where basic needs for food and shelter are not as prominently felt as they were in the older times or as they are felt in poorer countries. Need for a good companion has found a profound psychological value for the majority of people. The unfortunate reality is that the need for compassion is increasing, mostly because people are deprived of it more every day in our hectic social settings. It is also because they have less of it themselves to offer—since conceit has become a social norm. This crucial point requires further explanations, as offered in Chapter Ten under the topic of 'Need Urgency'.

Another useful implication of Diagram 8.3 is that even couples striving for their basic personal needs can possibly build a good relationship, even as high as SLove. Many other interesting points about the meaning of Diagram 8.3 are noted and discussed below.

'Relationship Needs Forest' Interpretation

Diagram 8.3 reveals many points consistent with our daily observations. The most significant interpretations are:

1. 'Companionship' is a basic need based on the discussions in this book (mainly Chapters 1 & 10). It is not just a social need.
2. Many types of balanced relationships exist, where partners agree on their relationship model, independence level, and personal needs that this model normally supports.

3. Personal needs and relationship needs are reconcilable if partners are mature and sincere about their needs and agree on the relationship model that best fits their personal lifestyle and authentic needs. All the points in Diagram 8.3 can fit a variety of personal preferences of most couples if partners in each relationship know exactly what each one wants, put them in their contract, and then honour their words.
4. Five relationship models are defined along the 'relationship success arrow' and explained in the next chapter.
5. All couples represented by a point in this diagram can relate somewhat effectively (passively or actively) to manage their relationships. Relationships that are dysfunctional for some reason normally induce too many conflicts to allow the kind of balance represented by the points in Diagram 8.3.
6. All the points in Diagram 8.3 represent those cases where partners' expectations (from their relationship) are somewhat satisfied by a certain relationship model, because, 1) their personal expectations are reasonable, 2) their relationship expectations somewhat coincide with their limited personal needs, and 3) they know the restrictions of the model they have chosen, and stay within its boundaries.
7. Regardless of the relationship model partners have chosen, they adhere to the relationship framework and GARP.
8. Thus, against common perception, many types of successful relationships exist if partners chose the right relationship model based on their personalities and needs.
9. The highlighted Success Arrow shows the most ideal types of relationships, because partners' personal needs coincide with their relationship needs perfectly. This arrow signifies 'Relationship Success,' as every point on the arrow reflects a perfect relationship. Partners have developed a successful balance in their relationship without allowing their personal needs jeopardize their relationship needs or sacrificing their personal needs too much.

10. Other points in the diagram (such as points A and Z) are less perfect, but still manageable, relationships. A is clearly a more successful relationship than Z.
11. Point A reflects the case where partners are more successful in their relationship than they are in achieving their personal needs. They have sacrificed some of their personal needs to improve their relationship.
12. Conversely, point Z reflects that partners have sacrificed some aspects of their relationship in order to pursue their personal goals.
13. Anyway, both points A and Z reflect working relationships, as long as partners continue their teamwork, adhere to the relationship model they have chosen, and know how much emphasis they wish to put on personal needs. Respecting the relationship contract they have signed and other aspects of the relationship framework would ensure that this agreed balance is kept. Thus, any disagreement can be attributed only to partners' incompatibility issues. The cases explained here are based on the assumptions that partners are rather compatible and have agreed on the relationship model.
14. Point A also indicates that these partners are probably not too ambitious. The reason is that, although partners can help each other to pursue their personal goals, they are somehow not using this opportunity to better themselves. They seem stuck with their basic needs (including social acceptance and security), their enthusiasms to keep each other happy, and their drives to make their relationship successful.
15. Point Z, on the other hand, reflects a relationship where partners' higher needs and ambitions are getting a priority. Thus, their relationship is not going to higher levels and they cannot depend on each other as much as couple A does. Couple Z is more distracted by personal needs such as work, friends, or even spirituality. Thus, they cannot give enough attention to each other and enhance their friendship. While

they are relating rather actively, their relationship is only fulfilling their needs for ELove and compassion.

16. The higher partners move up the Success Arrow, the more successful (complete) their relationship is, the stronger the bonding of partners is, and the more their personal needs are satisfied.
17. The higher levels in the tree, e.g., friendship, support partners better to achieve their personal needs. Still, we do not take advantage of this opportunity, since we are obsessed with our lower personal needs, such as rivalry, Elove, and greed. Our Ego stops us from seeing the larger picture; to cooperate for achieving our higher personal needs. The higher up we climb the relationship needs tree, a higher sense of partners' dependability and maturity is needed. Accordingly, people's rising urge for independence means that they should stick to relationship models in the lower levels.
18. In 'co-existence' (relationship model 1), partners can devote themselves totally to achieve their personal needs. This means that even couples who give the highest priority to personal needs and individualism could be in manageable relationships. In this model, merely minimum expectations are placed on partners, just to maintain their relationship in line with GARP and partners' initial contract. All partners should do is to make sure they have similar objectives and temperaments.
19. Moving up the relationship needs tree is not easy or a task that partners can negotiate on without first improving their personal mentalities. They must be truly mature in terms of personality, lifestyle, and priorities in order to move up to a higher level in the relationship needs tree. This progression is not by partners' desire or choice, but rather an automatic one, as a natural consequence of partners' compatibility, personality, and needs. Nevertheless, partners must feel and show they are actually ready for a higher dependency level.

20. Therefore, partners should be realistic about the relationship model they choose. Especially, newlyweds must choose the lowest relationship model at the beginning. They should not demand a high level of dependency until they are sure about their capacities to remain humble and free from Ego.

Although some or all of partners' unrealistic expectations (as shown in Table 4.2) can be satisfied by higher level models, those expectations should still reflect partners' natural needs, instead of egotistical whims or erratic demands. The minute partners' expectations are contaminated by their obsessions, raw demands, or a sense of manipulation and domination, the relationship model becomes dysfunctional. This applies even more strictly to higher-level relationship models. Obviously, forgiveness, tolerance, fairness, and flexibility to deal with our partners' obsessions and flaws are always helpful in reducing frictions. However, the more authentic partners' needs and demands are, the better would be their chances to climb up the 'relationship needs tree.' Nonetheless, partners' 'unrealistic expectations' should not imply or be linked with 'unauthentic needs.' The former refers to certain expectations that must not be normally sought by couples under most general conditions, although still likely at the higher levels of relationships' needs tree. Unauthentic needs, on the other hand, represent those demented desires and obsessions that are merely egotistical, thus never acceptable in any type of relationship.

"Then, can enough of us dogmatic, egotistical humans really balance our personal needs with relationship needs for making our lives and societies a bit more peaceful and functional, after all?" This is a timely, valid question to ask after all the talks in this chapter. Therefore, it is addressed in the next chapter.

Chapter Nine

Balancing Personal and Relationship Needs

These days, our sense of entitlement for endless love, sex, compassion, and material stuff have made us too needy and desperate—all in hopes of making our lives as complete as possible. We are suffocating in our marriages due to so many artificial needs that we have created in the recent decades and imposed on relationships, too, thus made them quite complex and stressful. Now, our personal needs and relationship needs are becoming more conflicting and troublesome every year, thus making our marriages too difficult to manage.

Another reason for so much conflict in relationships these days is that no longer any relationship principles exist to guide couples. Still, most couples imagine quite naively that they can start and maintain their relationships at the highest level of partners' dependency (as shown in the relationship needs tree —Model 5 on Page 143) automatically and fulfil its complex requirements. It is probably clear how illogical this expectation is and why family and social affairs are so chaotic.

Therefore, a main objective of the relationship framework is to *align partners' needs with relationships' generic needs,* so that marriages work smoother and healthier. Then again, this sacred mission is not even addressed or publicized in society.

Relationship Models

Table 9.1 lists the five grids shown in Diagram 8.3. Each grid represents a relationship type (model) according to a level of personal need for independence. The Success Arrow in that diagram represents models that can work most successfully.

A comprehensive discussion of the five models and their mechanisms for *relating* within various relationships is offered below. However, these descriptions are merely prototypes for providing enough insight about relationship models and their natures in general. Much more research and details about these models' characteristic, and possibly another 5-7 supplementary ones, require a separate book.

Table 9.1: Main Relationship Models

Relationship Model (Grid)	Relationship Needs Tree (Diagram 8.1)	Personal Needs Tree* (Diagram 8.2)
1	Co-existence	Food, Shelter, Sex**
2	Compassion/MLove	Security
3	Friendship/ELove	Social
4	Dependence/Success	Status, Ambitions
5	Devotion/SLove	Self-actualization

* This is based on Abraham Maslow's 'Personal Needs Hierarchy' Theorem.
** 'Need for Companion' may be shown in Grid 1, too, based on this book's theory.

Relationship Model 1: Co-existence

In this type of relationship, partners co-exist in the sense that their obligations towards each other are complete by fulfilling their needs for **food and shelter and sex** (and basic attention). This model offers a couple of interesting situations: **First,** partners have the highest level of independence to pursue their personal needs as long as the basic level of relationship need (Grid 1-Co-existence) is satisfied. Partners agree and succeed in co-existing without placing higher demands on each other. Partners' independence is emphasized, while they enjoy their marriage in a civilized manner. Thus, they have the chance to chase their highest personal aspirations without being bound or burdened by their partner's raw demands. This opportunity begins to diminish fast at the middle levels of the relationship tree, as partners place more demands on each other, and they should balance their needs for independence and dependence more precisely, too. Therefore, as relationship expectations rise, partners' ability to pursue their personal needs is restricted —a commonplace observation. They must give more attention to their partners and their relationship. Surely, the higher the expectations from relationships, the more critical and harder it gets to balance personal needs with the relationship needs.

The Success Arrow in Diagram 8.3 shows a solid balance between the relationship needs and personal needs of partners. The intersecting vertical and horizontal lines for each model become longer as we go up the relationship needs tree, which reflects the growing degree of difficulty to create a balance between the relationship needs and personal needs of partners as they move up on the Success Arrow. It also gets harder for partners to reach the required balance between their personal needs for dependence and independence.

The **second** implication of this relationship model is that even people satisfying only their basic needs (i.e., food and shelter) can reach the highest level in the relationship tree—even Slove—if they are humble and selfless (and are willing to devote themselves fully to their partners, instead of stressing on their personal needs and goals).

This is the most basic type of relating. Partners are familiar with the relationship framework and GARP. They are clear about their *contracted* expectations and stick to them. In this particular model, partners have not yet shown the capacity or interest to fulfil the higher-level needs of relationships, e.g., compassion and MLove. They might have wrong perceptions about each other and their relationship. However, the level of frictions is minimal, just because partners adhere to the basic guidelines of GARP and maintain low expectations from their relationship. Nonetheless, the fact that partners are still in this relationship shows that they have fulfilled some of the realistic expectations listed in Table 4.1, know how to respect each other, and behave civilly within 'the relationship framework.' In this model, partners are *relating passively.* While all the expectations in Table 4.1 are fulfilled at least at some minimal levels, the emphasis is only on certain basic expectations that are *urgently* required, such as sex, teamwork, independence, and communication.

Relationship Model 2: Compassion/MLove

In this type of relationship, partners are mainly looking for an added sense of **security** in their relationship. They expect their partners to show compassion, too, although it might not be sincere enough. The focus on 'security' might be a reflection of one or both partners' psychological or financial insecurity. They use some Model and MLove to relate and reflect passion and security. They wisely start their relationship with caution, try to keep certain boundaries, and curb their demands for too much attention (ELove). Their random attempt to fulfil more of their personal needs results in conflicts. In particular, if a partner attends to his/her social needs unilaterally, the other partner feels threatened or bored, thus arguments erupt. The basic balance in their relationship feels shaky and threatened if partners begin to move beyond their comfort zone too often. Therefore, they limit their pursuit of personal needs and stop nagging or asking for too much affection beyond MLove.

This is the most common relationship model that couples try to adopt (and the one that most couples are best capable of handling). In this kind of relationship, partners try to respond to some of their partners' need for compassion. They know how to adapt to relationship needs and pressures effectively and to express their emotions and needs productively. In the process, they satisfy each other's need for MLove—a sense of being loved. They are still *relating rather passively*, but they know how to maintain their relationship boundaries and not hurt each other's feelings. They try to curb their urges to force their opinions or needs. The additional expectations fulfilled in this model more *urgently* are: security, compassion, MLove, peace, and a higher sense of cooperation.

Relationship Model 3: Friendship/ELove

In this type of relationship, partners relate more constructively with a focus on **friendship**. Thus, they find the strength and motivation to satisfy some of their unrealistic needs such as Elove, too. Friendship also gives them a higher capacity for tolerance, teamwork, and making compromises. They support each other's needs and goals more actively. They explore their personal needs and enjoy their independent social interactions without their actions coming across too threatening for their relationship. They use Model and MLove more effectively to express their emotions, boost their friendship, and raise their relationship's quality.

In this relationship model, people get a chance to fulfil their social needs fully. Still, they might feel some limitations to pursue their more advanced personal goals without threatening their relationships' stability. They might find the challenge of aligning their dependence and independence needs difficult occasionally, but overall they have a good grasp of them.

In this kind of relating, partners are able to show even more compassion and relate better. They know how to satisfy each other's needs somewhat effectively and how to be true friends. They are also able and willing to satisfy some of their partners' (unrealistic) needs in Table 4.2 as well, e.g., ELove. Although ELove is an unrealistic expectation in relationships, it helps in developing relationships when it is partially satisfied (through partners' friendship and adaptation). Their friendship's strength actually helps them respond to some of each other's unrealistic demands for attention and ELove. In this model, partners are *relating rather actively*. The additional expectations satisfied in this model more *urgently* are: basic dependency, friendship, ELove, and a preliminary sense of commitment.

Relationship Model 4: Dependence/Personal Success

In this type of relationship, partners have proven their maturity to align their personal and relationship needs. The emphasis is on **supporting** each other to fulfil their personal ambitions. They also align their dependence and independence needs more effectively. Thus, a higher sense of mutual dependence erupts naturally, while partners feel enough sense of independence as well. The joy of companionship empowers partners to follow and accomplish even their high aspirations, while maintaining a fulfilling relationship, too.

In this kind of relationship, partners are in harmony with each other. They are *relating actively*. They can truly rely on each other and contribute effectively to each other's personal goals. They know how to support each other compassionately to succeed in their personal pursuits. The added expectations satisfied in this model more *urgently* are: high dependence, personal success, commitment, and longevity.

Relationship Model 5: SLove

This is the most successful, complex, and complete type of relationship. It empowers partners to reach enlightenment, tranquility, **SLove**, and they relate naturally. At the same time, getting here has definitely not been easy or quick!

Reaching this highest level of achievement in a relationship demonstrates partners' wisdom, maturity, compassion, and the kind of complex artistry that most humans fail to even taste. Accordingly, this is the level where partners become true soul mates. They relate most positively and actively emotionally, effectively, and efficiently. This gives partners the opportunity to feel and satisfy their spirituality needs and everything else that one could ideally expect from a relationship. They reach love that is heavenly, selfless, and eternal. In this sacred model, all the expectations in both Tables 4.1 and 4.2 are satisfied. Partners are totally relating. *Hooray!!*

For a relationship to flourish and succeed, partners must have high personal qualities, recognize their quirks, and learn the demands for being in any of the above relationship models. Some mechanisms and 'relating' techniques also help couples succeed in their specific relationship model once they adopt the relationship framework and principles noted throughout this book. Discussing all the details about relationship models' mechanisms and means of moving up to the higher levels is beyond the scope of this book, but they might be addressed in another book as part of the Love and Relationship series.

The 'relationship needs tree' and the relationship models presented in this book are simple prototypes for the purpose of introducing plausible solutions for our faltering relationships. However, these simple models can be expanded and explained in a full-fledged working manual possibly with a relationship tree that supports probably a dozen models. Couples can use that manual to identify the specific type of relationship that suits them. Those relationship models can provide many types of successful relationships that we could reasonably conceive. Couples could use the manual and possibly a questionnaire to identify the suitable relationship model for them by matching their personalities and needs to the requirements of various models. The characteristics and requirements of the models would be easy to understand and follow.

Diagram 8.3 can also be expanded to show the mechanism of aligning personal and relationship needs in more detail. This can further facilitate couples' ability to choose the kind of balance they like to create. Eventually, all these details will be fully explored and available for the lucky couples of the 22nd century. Developing these concepts and models is just another type of radical change in relationship and social mechanisms that we need, i.e., the topic that will be presented in Chapter Eleven. Meanwhile, we all can take small steps, change our mindsets, participate in propagating the new ideas, and learn some of the tricks suggested in this book for improving our relationships right away.

Luckily, it seems plausible that 5 to 12 relationship models can accommodate the majority of relationships. They can help couples relate actively or passively, satisfy a majority of the relationship needs, and stir a relationship environment where the three Es (emotions, effectiveness and efficiency) can be encouraged and achieved at some degrees.

As stressed enough already, relationship models should be developed by experts, so that most couples can choose the best models for them mainly based on the degree of dependence and independence they need and demand for their relationship. Therefore, to grasp the importance of relationship models and the intricacy of people's strong needs for both dependence and independence, readers might like to review this topic (people's need for dependence and independence) in this author's two books, *The Nature of Love and Relationships,* and *Gender Qualities, Quirks, and Quarrels*.

Chapter Ten

Need Urgency

'Personal needs tree' is a scientific principle used in this book to compare with relationships needs for building the five relationship models in Chapter Nine. 'Personal need urgency' is a related scientific concept that requires some analysis, too, due to its effects on relationships' health. Partners' obsessions for stressing on some personal ambitions (needs) somewhat contrary to a general format suggested in the Maslow's needs tree cause additional clashes between them. Need urgency theory is also useful for measuring partners' compatibilities.

Need Urgency Implications

According to Maslow, people try intuitively to satisfy their basic needs, starting with 'shelter and food,' before moving up to the next group (level) of needs. That is, they concentrate on their needs in some logical order. The theory also stipulates that if a person's lower needs are disrupted swiftly, he/she moves down the needs tree again. He/she would have to fulfil those lower needs before climbing back up the tree again.

Yet, the need urgency concept adds a bizarre dimension to Maslow's general theorem. It presents cases where a person's urgent (often artificial) need (unique ambition) disregards his/

her orderly upward or downward tendencies. Before discussing the implications of people's need urgencies in modern societies, a few examples about this concept can help:

1. Overachievers usually ignore their lower needs, e.g., social or security, since their need for success feels too urgent and crucial for them. They are so obsessed with self-actualizing endeavours they might stop caring about their social needs, security, or even food. People with this mentality are plenty in society at all levels of needs hierarchy. They sacrifice their lives, families, and basic needs in order to fulfil their unique urges, ideologies, or spiritual missions on earth.
2. We expect companionship to fall in the category of social needs on Maslow's needs hierarchy. However, in reality, this is not the case, especially in the present social setting. We are too needy for compassion and companionship these days. Sometimes, even a starving homeless might prefer a companion to food or shelter. This is an example of our psychological and physiological urgent needs competing for attention. A person overwhelmed by love might stop caring about food or security. Some even commit suicide for love or political ideologies. A person's 'psychological construct' usually determines the urgency of his/her needs. This may be a permanent condition or a temporary setback. Thus, the 'need urgency' concept suggests that for many of us being at a certain level of the needs tree is so urgent we can ignore all other needs. This condition is often referred to as obsession, but could have other sources, too, such as addiction, fanaticism, false pride, etc. Some people crave 'social acceptance' or 'status' more than tranquility even when they know that their health and happiness depends on tangible personal achievements and 'self-actualization'.
3. Ambitious people (or workaholics) actually realize, and suffer from, the lack of enough time to attend to their social life or family. Still they cannot bring themselves to change their priorities. Their ambitions and egotistical needs stop

them from spending enough time on self-development and spiritual reflections.

4. Artists and scholars know they are missing a good slice of life and all the fun out there. They get over-conscious and anxious about their choices. Still, their need for creativity prevents them from wasting time on anything else.
5. Sometimes, we settle for friends and companions who are not up to our standards or compatible with us. We do this because of our urgent need to socialize or elude loneliness, instead of waiting for a perfect friend or partner.
6. Even reaching the height of Maslow's needs tree does not guarantee lasting tranquility. For one thing, self-actualizers must create new things regularly to keep the actualization cycle alive and potent. On some occasions, they might not be happy even at the height of their creativity. So many reasons exist for this; for example, when they do not get the recognition they think they deserve. In all, satisfying our needs, even self-actualization, would not automatically turn into happiness or freedom from our erratic needs. This condition might cause stress, confusion, and a motive to change our need priorities and urgencies.

Need urgency usually indicates the *intensity* of a certain need, too, like an obsession, which might even lead to insanity. This is a rather prevalent condition in society, thus the cause of many relationship conflicts and fights. For instance, a partner may be obsessed with socializing. He/she is happy only when friends or family are around. This need may cause a major conflict, especially when the other partner prefers a quieter lifestyle. People are often too absorbed in their obsessions to consider them excessive or unnatural. Therefore, they argue about the sources of tension in their relationships uselessly. Some people have an obsession for shopping or controlling everything and everyone. Like some kind of addiction, these need urgencies or obsessions can drain the person and people around him/her. Even a simple obsession for cleanliness or tidiness can quickly override love when partners start to get on each other's nerves. And then we keep insisting that love alone can hold our relationships together!

Partners' need urgencies are short or long term depending on circumstances. It could manifest in terms of mood swings or a complete change of one's lifestyle altogether. Usually partners even fall out of love quickly, because of their sudden obsession to pursue a new priority, e.g., to get the university degree they had left incomplete thirty years before. Or a swift sense of urgency to reclaim one's identity, or attend to one's awakened ambitions. These types of sudden need urgencies damage the relative balance within a relationship. Partners suddenly face an unfamiliar and intimidating atmosphere and they do not know how to deal with it. In particular, sudden need urgencies (obsessions) for some fanciful objectives, e.g., finding more love, sexuality, or happiness often ruin many relationships, *because we keep thinking and saying that life is too short and we live only once!*

Mood swings are the outcome of need urgencies shifting from one thing to another rather quickly and illogically. Often, they are simply the outcome of a partner's defence mechanism trying to cope with relationship conundrums or to retaliate. Another reason is that couples often get tired of the status quo or their partners. Thus, they invent an urgent need to escape boredom and depression. The change is often also radical and drastic, since it must overcome their boredom or irritate their partners. Under these conditions, partners appear neurotic and irrational to each other. Their relationship remains unbalanced, too, because partners have difficulty grasping the meaning and purpose of each other's erratic needs and moods. They do not know what has caused them, when they might reappear, and how to react to them. This is a prevalent situation considering people's highly emotional need urgencies, nowadays, as well as their oversensitivity. This kind of relationship environment heightens partners' confusion, misperceptions, and frustration.

Most of these need urgencies are psychological and impulsive, thus hard to deal with.

Need urgency shows people's psychological construct. For some people, their need urgency reflects a deep-rooted, lasting obsession that haunts them throughout their lives. This is a static type of need urgency, e.g., obsession for cleanliness or an artist's need for self-actualization. It is a reflection of one's personality. This type of permanent obsession is at least stable and predictable. Partners can learn to either live with these types of obsessions or get out of the relationship. However, often, need urgencies are the symptoms of partners' mood swings and self-defence. These types of erratic behaviour are more difficult to deal with.

Sometimes, people's need urgencies feel critically pressing or time-restrained, too, e.g., to pursue one's ambitions or have children before a certain age. In the new era, the urgency to find a better relationship than the existing one is becoming a time-restrained, pressing need, too. Especially, when a person is getting old or has left a relationship, he/she suddenly feels an urgent need to find love in a new companion at all cost as soon as possible. The fear of loneliness suddenly makes him/her anxious. The need for a companion finds an exceptionally high urgency. He/she applies Model relentlessly and sacrifices many other personal needs to satisfy this urgent need as soon as possible. Sometimes, a person is so desperate he/she looks totally lost and pathetic.

As a whole, another complexity of relationships lies in the fact that people's unique need urgencies (obsessions) usually do not follow any logic. They go up or down the personal needs tree quickly without any specific order or reason. Time-restrained urgencies (e.g., an urge to be loved again) obviously are quite stressful for the person and people around him/her. Besides lifestyle and personality differences of partners, their unpredictable need urgencies and obsessions often clash and create many additional conflicts in relationships.

Need Urgency's Impact on Relationships

The above examples and cases show how our 'need urgencies' distort the principles of Maslow's personal needs hierarchy. More importantly, they demonstrate how our 'need urgencies' destabilize our relationships A few other general points about the effect of need urgency should also be mentioned briefly here. **First,** as noted before, the need for a companion appears to impose a special urgency on our lives. All of our 'personal needs' demand our attention at some degree and time. Yet, the need for a companion seems to be an everlasting and imposing one. It seems to place the highest level of urgency throughout our lives. In fact, our other personal needs often appear pale and inconsequential compared with our need for a companion. Our emotional needs put the highest psychological demand on our existence. **Thus, finding solutions for our relationship issues has become an urgent matter for modern societies.**

Second, partners' 'need urgencies' taint their compatibility, and thus their relationships' health. This happens when one or both partners remain uncertain about their expectations from their relationship and their true personal needs. When they cannot align their personal and relationship needs, they feel a lingering tension, which then hurts their relationship as well. Thus, partners should convince themselves personally of their needs' authenticity and their relationship model's suitability for them. Any phony balance would only hurt them personally and collectively. They must be flexible, but not at the expense of sacrificing their natural personal needs or realistic expectations from their relationship, all for the sake of fitting themselves into a special relationship model. They must negotiate to find a clear, sensible position for themselves on the 'relationship needs tree.' And they should feel truly comfortable with that compromise and the relationship model they have adopted. Since partners' need urgencies affect their compatibility vastly, **assessing their need urgencies is another crucial factor for**

gauging couples' compatibility. At the same time, couples must remember that since their need urgencies vary, their mood and attitude changes would affect their relationships adversely. Usually their own or their partner's need urgencies should be changed to create a rather balanced status in their relationship.

Third, assessing partners' need urgencies is an important factor for measuring their compatibility and choosing the right relationship model. Although couples must have the option of choosing the best relationship model based on their needs and personality, **partners should always start with the simplest relationship model, which is the lowest on the relationship tree–with a low level of dependency on their partner.** They could then strive to climb up the tree according to their need urgencies, actual experiences in their relationship, and by showing their maturity and personality strengths. The policy to start from the lowest level of the relationship tree must replace our existing mentality to start at the highest level. This would be a substantial social challenge.

Fourth, some instinctual needs stir deep need urgencies in relationships and cause major havoc, as explained below.

The Impact of Instinctual Needs

The impact of our instinctual needs on decision-making and social encounters is enormous, as they are the least tameable needs. More importantly, instinctual urges find a high urgency in our personal lives and relationships. The roles that five of these types of needs play in our relationships are particularly immense. They are the needs for: 1) Control, 2) Sex, 3) Love, 4) Dependence, and 5) Independence.

These needs become too urgent in almost all relationships, nowadays. Yet, it is not clear how they fall within the overall 'personal needs tree' of Maslow. In the context of Maslow's model, 'need for control' might be considered a symptom of personal need for security. 'Need for sex' might be seen as a basic physiological need. As explained before, our conflicting needs for dependence and independence actually seem to be impacting our perceptions of all our other needs. 'Need for love' seems to be driven by many other personal needs, as it manifests in terms of ELove, MLove, and SLove. Anyway, the real implications of the above instinctual needs are quite complex. More importantly, it is their roles in relationships that are of interest in this book, e.g., when two partners end up using sex as a mechanism for retaliation or manipulating each other. Or in the manner individuals' need for independence impacts their relationships in such a wide spectrum, especially regarding partners' need for compassion and dependence. It appears that these types of instinctual needs have found a true urgency and importance in relationships in the new era. As such, companionship is no longer a 'social need' on Maslow's needs tree. Rather, it is an essential (basic) need as claimed in this book.

These essential needs and their impact on relationships are reviewed in detail in this author's books, *The Nature of Love and Relationships* and *Gender Qualities, Quirks, and Quarrels.*

Need Setback Hysteria

Maslow's 'personal needs hierarchy' implies that normal people go about satisfying their needs in a civilized, orderly manner. They are content with the level of personal needs they have satisfied so far, while looking forward to the next level on the tree with patience, objectivity, and a sound plan. It is assumed that people are rational and set their expectations according to their abilities and efforts. Surely, moving up the personal needs hierarchy and satisfying a higher-level need is not easy. Still, traditionally and logically, we do not expect people to get too anxious when their higher needs are not yet satisfied. These days, however, people are too sensitive about achieving some ambitious or imaginary goals that they feel entitled to.

Therefore, the atmosphere for need fulfilment is no longer calm and logical, nowadays. In particular, with all the hoopla in society for getting rich and famous quickly, the price of not satisfying personal needs has grown too high. Everybody has become overambitious now, because society pushes the idea that everybody can become whoever they want to be and have everything they wish if they just put their minds into it. So, people have become too obsessive with their goals and needs to get rich fast, at least for not been seen as a fool or failure! Everybody is looking for a shortcut to have more things with less work, and to get a lot of sympathy even when they are too arrogant themselves. Positive thinking and the childish slogan about everybody's ability to achieve any goal have screwed up people's minds, too. They set unrealistic goals for themselves and treat them as legitimate needs.

The need to prove one's individuality is further pushing people to set fanciful goals for themselves. They are hoping to make their so-called individualism manifest through fame, wealth, and recognition. Their needs for identity and success have combined and turned into an epidemic obsession for the public. They perceive all kinds of fantasies, especially for fame and wealth, as their imperative (basic) needs. In all, people just keep creating more artificial needs for themselves every year. To make the matter worse, many people see these fantasies as 'urgent needs' that should take precedence over many other normal life objectives.

Since a large portion of population cannot accomplish their exaggerated plans and whims, they feel frustrated, distressed, and unappreciated. They take their failures too deeply to heart. They feel incomplete, a total fool or failure, and unworthy. Both at the personal level and in relationships, the unattained goals are taken as catastrophes and shameful. Simple matters that were traditionally considered inconsequential for personal welfare or relationships' health have now turned into a source of major frustration and hysteria. People's reactions are often too drastic. They store deep inner hurts and hostility. They get hysterical. They might even show signs of insanity when a simple need remains unfulfilled. Their oversensitivity about their unfulfilled needs is drastic, nowadays. Thus, the level of psychological insecurity, frustration, anger, and crimes is rising in society due to people's growing inner conflicts.

In all, the kind of graceful contentment and orderly growth of personal needs, as is rather suggested by Maslow's personal needs tree, is no longer prevalent. On the contrary, we witness people's big hysteria for failing to climb up the personal needs tree fast enough. The author refers to this emerging epidemic as Need Setback Hysteria—NSH. Our need urgencies and obsessions make the matter of NSH even more troublesome.

NSH is particularly evident and harmful in relationships, since couples start with high expectations. They dream about so many of their desires becoming magically fulfilled through their magnificent relationships and by their intelligent, faithful partners' devotion. When they face their partners' humanistic inability to respond to all their demands and high expectations, they react hysterically and make life miserable for themselves and their partners. It also occurs when couples keep imagining and choosing relationship models beyond their mental abilities. Often, they imagine some kind of a relationship arrangement that cannot fit within any of the practical models presented in this book, anyway.

Nevertheless, while couples' seemingly urgent (fanciful) needs (NU) are growing constantly, their hysteria (NSH) and frustration have raised personal stress level and caused more chaos in society.

Chapter Eleven
Radical Solutions

The complexity of relationships is easy to grasp when we study the intricacies of human nature. We might notice how hopelessly helpless we humans are due to our psychological defects and social corruption. We realize our deep entrapment within societies' vile values and our soiled personality aspects, e.g., Ego, Model, Self. We are driven by our misperceptions, our conscience and desires, and our needs and deprivations. So, at the end, we face a confusing and complex life even if we knew how to be, and lived as, an independent person.

A relationship gets two times more complex if we add up the idiosyncrasies of two partners making the relationship. In fact, the complexity of relationships increases beyond the sum of the two partners' idiosyncrasies, as their interactions create many additional levels of resistance and contradictions. Many new dimensions and limitations emerge in relationships and partners' lives beyond their personal limits and experiences. Even their dormant idiosyncrasies pop out of nowhere. They might even get an urge to kill (themselves and others) due to their deep frustration and helplessness infesting their minds so deeply. In particular, when two partners' Egos and Models interact and incite one another, they introduce a much wider range of potential problems for themselves and other people.

Considering the gloomy prospect of relationships without a 'relationship framework,' marriage counsellors' and scholars' advices seem unproductive, if not futile altogether, nowadays, too. The reason is that without proper mindsets and knowledge of a reliable relationship framework, partners cannot relate to each other effectively and efficiently. To really help couples, a counsellor or a writer must show them how to relate according to certain guidelines similar to what this book is proposing for a relationship framework. S/he must first explain how couples could relate, for what objectives, and how to minimize their expectations to achieve those goals. These topics must actually be taught in high schools and colleges. Instead, most marriage counsellors increase couples' expectations from relationships by giving them the impression that they should (and could) rekindle romance to save their relationship by role-playing. However, giving couples false hopes about finding their lost loves, or overcoming their mistrusts, cannot help them. It only delays partners' objective decisions about the viability of their relationship. It is rather naïve to believe MLove alone can make couples relate, even if they had the talent and patience to sustain the role-playing requirements of MLove.

Instead, relationship counsellors could explain, and work with, the **reality** of relationships in the new era. They can help couples perceive and adopt one of two feasible options: to stay together with lower expectations, or get out of the relationship. Counsellors and authors are trying to help couples make the best of their relationships. Yet, they do not have a uniform method or model to show the requirements of relationships in the new era. They have not yet agreed on a set of principles and a relationship framework for couples to follow. Naturally, the idea of couples following certain guidelines might sound laughable already for two reasons at least: 1) People are too erratic, emotional, selfish, and lazy (among many other quirks) to submit to any type of order and principles easily. 2) Our societies are advocating individualism and self-image in line with a crude notion about people's democratic rights. Sadly, this mentality reduces people's appetite for general principles and raises incongruity, conflict, and chaos among people.

Obviously, the successful implementation of a relationship framework depends on partners' moods and personalities. It depends on their abilities to manage their own Egos and bear their partners'. Couples must be highly talented team players. However, we know that human nature and their conditioned personalities cannot be readily changed. *Managing their own Egos and tolerating their partners'* require lots of efforts, awareness, and sacrifice by both partners. Still, knowing the truth regarding the reality of relationships in the modern world might by itself help partners choose a viable option for them. Perhaps it would shake them out of their fantasy world about relationships and realize the naivety of their expectations. This knowledge alone might help them find a better way of *relating* to their partners and keeping their relationship, if it is worth keeping. They might at least try to find a different relationship model to help them relate without a need to separate.

Even a simple admission about people's difficulty to refit their personalities and lower their expectations from life and relationships might motivate partners to ponder their options about a companion more realistically. This basic knowledge can expedite both their self-awareness and adaptation process. Meanwhile, they might adopt a flexible mentality to separate civilly when they can no longer relate emotionally, effectively, or efficiently—the 'three-E' factors of relating.

Sadly, finding relationship solutions is immensely urgent and would require radical changes in social mechanisms and people's mentalities. In fact, before delving into this author's suggestions, it seems appropriate to quote Elizabeth Gilbert's witty and succinct observation in her book, *Committed*. I am quoting it here from memory, which is quite close, if not the exact, wording she has used to refer to the hectic setting of relationships in the new era:

> *"I'm surprised that they (governments) are still allowing us to get married!"*

The point is that we all rather agree that when the society at large faces a major challenge, we hope that some authority (usually the government in democratic societies) steps in to at least play the role of a moderator and induce order before a catastrophe cripples the whole socioeconomic structure. Let us hope we do not have to wait for the boiling point where the government is forced to restrict marriages! Instead, we need the government's and scholar's intervention to bring objectivity back into relationships somehow, because religions and old cultures cannot play that role anymore. Companionship is an immensely important facet of social structure and should not be left unattended for so long.

Surely, the radical solutions suggested in this chapter sound absurd, unromantic, and even offensive to some people. Thus, it is stressed that the ultimate objective of this book, especially these 'radical solutions,' is to explore practical options for our relationships. This book has little value for those who believe that the current situation is fine. Yet, for those of us concerned about future generations, many radical changes in our social and personal mentalities seem inevitable to elude the need for ultra radical options (e.g., open marriage). We need practical principles before desperate options overwhelm us and become an epidemic, just for tolerating our marriages one more day. We merely need open-minded marriages, not open marriages.

Need for a Fresh Mentality

Relationships will always remain a demanding and confusing aspect of human existence. More depressing, however, they have become incredibly instable, nowadays. Thus, we should begin to see and accept relationships in a different light from what we are accustomed to as a lasting union. It takes lots of courage and effort to prepare ourselves for a possible collapse of our marriages. Even harder, we should also learn humility and modify our life values. We must build objectivity to assess our relationship practically, and often even decide to stay in it despite its emotional burdens. Finding manageable means of relating (maybe even passively) in imperfect relationships and boosting our tolerance level need lots of devotion and artistry. Then again, if partners are unwilling or unable to extend these efforts and sacrifices, in terms of observing the boundaries of the relationship framework, the only wise solution is to not marry or separate quickly if necessary. Otherwise, expecting things to improve and relationships stay manageable only by chance is just wasting time and goodwill.

Obviously, the option of not having a relationship sounds ridiculous, as seclusion does not fulfil any purpose, at least for the large majority of the population who seeks a companion as a basic need. Both our instincts and culture constantly force us to attend to this need actively. Thus, at least we need a trained mindset to bear the pressures of being in a relationship. The particular relationship model we choose should keep our egos, affairs, and communications manageable, while allowing us to deal with our personal needs individually. We either accept an imperfect situation, or do not. Our resistance to choose either of these two logical options—i.e., live it or leave it somewhat peacefully and logically—demonstrates only humans' level of stubbornness. We like to impose our needs on relationships and we wish to force our juvenile desires and perceptions on a concept so incapable of matching our wild imaginations. In this sense, our raw ideals about relationships are bound to give us only agony and hardship. In the present relationship setting, partners have no definite direction or prospect to look forward to. Therefore, something must be done; that *something* is the ultimate goal of a relationship framework. Yet, initially, we all need new mentalities in line with topics addressed throughout this book with a recap provided in Table 11.1 next page.

Table 11.1: Main Adjustments to Couples' Mentalities

1. Partners must reduce their expectations from marriage a lot.
2. Partners must know the specific relationship expectations and needs (listed in Tables 4.1, 4.2, and 4.3) before entering relationships. They should also be mentally equipped and willing to observe these relationship needs and expectations.
3. Partners must learn, and be willing, to relate to each other within the boundaries of the relationship framework (Table 5.1). They should identify the relationship model that best fits their needs and personalities (Diagram 9.3).
4. Partners must view relationships as a tentative arrangement, unless they do all the right things (which would be rather unlikely for most people).
5. Partners should be prepared to leave their relationships with open mind, without fuss or retaliation and before they start to hate each other.
6. Partners should view their relationship as an independent entity like a business enterprise. The concept of R-entity.
7. Couples should remember that love, ethics, and religion are not reliable mechanisms for authenticating or protecting their relationships. The vows exchanged in those settings are good only for glamorizing our feelings and ceremonies.
8. Couples should rely on their initial contracts to resolve their financial and custodial squabbles according to their sensible commitments to one another at the outset. The government role about such matters should be minimized.

Despite the ongoing struggles in relationships and clues about the futility of our imaginary expectations, sadly most of us do not seem to grasp the root of our relationship problems and just keep increasing our demands. We just keep torturing one another until death do us part. Under this circumstance, the only chance to gain some tranquility and free our spirits is to accept the realistic (and partly sad) options of relationships (i.e., living it or leaving it more peacefully and logically). It would help to broaden our minds about what relationships can be, what we can expect from them realistically, how and why. We must grasp the reality of relationships truly and much less selfishly. At the same time, adjustments are also needed in social mechanisms that support family relationships in society.

Need for New Social Mechanisms

To improve the state of relationships, social mechanisms must be revamped as well to propagate a new mentality in line with the values and lifestyles we crave. So far, societies have been dealing only with the symptoms of marriage failures, instead of realizing and responding to the underlying, deep problems of modern relationships. We are still ignoring the fact that new social values and mechanisms, including legal system, have brought us only more agony, stress, and disorder. *Overall, for improving partners' ability to relate effectively, relationship principles and environment must be entirely reassessed and redesigned.*

For identifying the needed new social mechanisms, we should first understand the social trends and major changes in lifestyles. They reflect people's mentalities and personal needs, which then affect their behaviours in their relationships.

The major social trends listed in Table 11.2 clearly reveal the sad fate of our relationships unless we act quickly. They demonstrate that we need a new relationship culture to help couples relate actively, or at least productively, in a somewhat passive setting. We should review the existing environment seriously and adjust our mentalities. We need corresponding mechanisms, too, to both encourage and handle the new social mentality. Both the public and governments have major social responsibilities to find means of working together according to novel, practical ideas for developing a relationship framework and guidelines. People also have the responsibility of pushing their leaders to help with revamping social mechanisms.

Table 11.2: Major New Social Trend

1. Social complexities, egotism, sexuality, personal needs, and phony values have been rising irrationally. Accordingly, relationships are becoming too cumbersome and superficial to define and tolerate.
2. People's expectations from relationships have also grown erratically. They consider relationship needs just an extension of their personal needs and a means of finding happiness.
3. People's stress level keeps growing due to socioeconomic and career demands as well as relationship conflicts.
4. Nowadays, people find their relationships too intolerable compared with, i) what they had initially imagined and, ii) how our ancestors felt even two generations ago.
5. People's inner conflicts and agonies keep increasing due to a sense of loneliness and insecurity, whether they have a partner or not.
6. People's needs for both independence and dependence keep rising. Thus, couples find fewer grounds to relate and work as a team.
7. The rate of relationship failures will continue to climb as people's personal needs and social complexity increase.
8. Each partner sees his/her individuality and independence the most important needs, both in and outside of his/her relationship. They consider themselves too important and deserving to live a happy life. If relationships hinder these needs in any manner, they choose their welfare above that of their partners' and relationships'. They leave if their high aspirations are hindered. Even worse, they often leave their relationships merely according to some idiotic personal obsessions or raw assumptions about the purpose of relationships.
9. Considering the above facts, couples' commitments to their partners and relationships is at best conditional. They stay in a relationship only if their partner can satisfy all their personal needs and keep them happy, while their tolerance level declines fast, too.
10. People gauge their relationships' health based on raw perceptions and misleading values, because no principles exist, nowadays, to guide their relationship or judge their health.
11. People's current approaches and attitudes fuel social deterioration, while they face more conflicts in their relationships and become more impatient, too, mostly due to rising social chaos.
12. The above trends are entangled collectively in a vicious cycle that is spinning out of control. Therefore, we should expect more of all the above facts in the years to come.

The main adjustments required to keep up with the social trends in Table 11.2 are mainly government's responsibility. These required social mechanisms are listed in Table 11.3 in line with the needed mental adjustments for people noted in Table 11.1. Collectively, these personal and social adjustments present a progressive perspective for relationships to fit our modern, radical mentality.

Mostly governments, educational entities, and legal systems should be responsible for developing and propagating social mechanisms, but the public's role to make this happen is even more important. The public and scholars must get seriously involved in pushing these progressive ideas.

Table 11.3: Main Adjustments to Social Mechanisms

Governments, educational institutions, and legal systems, as well as the public and scholars, must support and:

1. Spread the modern fad for individuality and independence *for proper purposes*.
2. Participate in all kinds of research to boost the quality of a 'relationship framework' and principles for the new era.
3. Teach the modern 'relationship framework' to the public in detail, especially at high schools.
4. Propagate the concept of R-entity – the idea of viewing marriages as an independent entity like a business enterprise.
5. Teach the concept of time-bounded marriages in society and legal systems.
6. Limit government's role in financial and custodial decisions.
7. Propagate the idea of partners' financial autonomy and responsibility, instead of relying on court system actively.

Surely, achieving everything listed in Tables 11.1 and 11.3 seem too idealistic. Even the very first condition in Table 11.1 (reducing personal expectations) is tough for everybody. Yet, people would eventually realize that changing their mentalities and reducing their expectations is the only way to strengthen their relationships and enrich their personal lives, too. Many couples are already making some ultra-radical changes in their mentalities, such as accepting open marriage as an option for enduring their messy relationships. These extremes are neither practical nor ethical. They would only make us sicker and more desperate.

The fact that couples go to these extremes in our so-called modern societies is actually the best clue that we urgently need some moderate changes in our mentalities about relationships.

It is a fact that people's real needs are undermined these days by existing socioeconomic mechanisms. For example, while looking for tranquility, people are encouraged to pursue wasteful lifestyles. Our political and socioeconomic systems have failed miserably. All the mechanisms developed within these systems have proven inept or careless, not to mention our leaders, greedy executives of major institutions, the police, religions, stock exchange, court system, educational entities, medical doctors and dentist, and all the rest of them. These social mechanisms bring us only more stress and depression, instead of tranquility. Relying on this incompetent setting to sort out our gloomy relationship mechanisms has proven quite inefficient, too. Therefore, we should try to at least minimize our reliance on these systems for sorting out our relationship needs and emotional conundrums.

The suggestions in Table 11.3 are reviewed in the following pages briefly, with the objective of developing plausible social mechanisms and radical solutions.

1. **Support and propagate the modern fad for individuality and independence *for proper purposes*.**

Laws and social mechanisms are supposed to be in line with people's needs. In the last few decades, however, our personal and relationship needs have skyrocketed without governments having an opportunity to adapt their mechanisms with these new needs. The main hurdle is that people's fast-expanding needs (e.g., for identity and independence) remain ambiguous even to them, as they strive relentlessly for some imaginary freedom and happiness. Too many misperceptions have tainted people's minds and raised their expectations from relationships and life. For example, while couples insist on independence, they want governments to protect their rights in relationships. This might not come across as a contradiction. However, it is, if we gauge its practical implications. First of all, we know that so many of relationship quarrels and breakdowns these days are caused by partners' obsession for individualism and materialism. People have also become too sensitive and get offended quickly when their Egos are bruised even slightly. And we feel incomplete and gloomy when our lifestyle is not as perfect as our daydreams. Thus, we imagine a happier life with a different partner. We abandon our relationships rather fast when we imagine it is not giving us enough independence, sex, or luxury. Yet, we play the role of compromising and modest partners during courtship. We conceal our greed and our overzealousness for independence, because they are not such flattering attributes to brag about. We do not want to put off our partner early on. The point is that if couples did not rely on courts to grant them financial compensation for being in a relationship, their true mentality would transpire early on before entering their relationships and so many couples would not end up in bad relationships based on trust and hope.

Many individuals still view their relationships as a source of financial security and reliance on someone else's struggle for money, while at the same time they emphasize on their independence in relationships. There is definitely some kind of inconsistency in cases like these. For this group at least, the existing rule to split the assets of partners 50/50 (or something like that) after separation is hypocritical. This is an example of governments' lack of initiative to deal with financial matters of relationships more fairly and realistically. This rule alone, in the author's opinion, is a major cause of so many separations in the new era. When a partner realizes the amount of money s/he can get by terminating a relationship, 'or just for punishing his/her crooked partner, s/he just cannot ignore the opportunity and luxury of separating. Thus, the government is indirectly responsible for too many hasty separations. The existing asset distribution mechanism during divorce is a foolish copout. It has evolved only because courts are not equipped to make a fair, comprehensive review of relationship variables, including its finances and partners' efforts. People and governments are careless about the confusions and damages (both financial and emotional) caused by present social mechanisms.

In recent decades, social mechanisms have been modified only to handle the *symptoms* of relationship failures, instead of the dire effects of changes in lifestyles and couples' mentalities. Courts have settled financial and child-custody matters with mediocre results, yet social mechanisms are not addressing the evolving relationship needs and couples' growing, rampant expectations in modern societies. People's mindsets, especially at the end of their once precious marriages, are causing a huge social and family mayhem, thus require an urgent attention by both people and legal systems.

Of course, it is hard to find the right social mechanisms when citizens' needs remain cluttered even for themselves. Couples do not know how to go about figuring out their true needs in a society besieged by consumerism and phony means of happiness. Superficial needs have tainted relationships and couples are not scientists to sort them out. They just feel those needs since everybody else around them feels the same needs and pushes the same values in their relationships. Meanwhile, the government is already too busy with urgent socioeconomic matters to worry about the real causes of relationship failures. Thus, it just deals with the symptoms of this social chaos the best it can at a high cost to taxpayers. Governments are just waiting idly by for the path of history to define the relationship needs eventually. In a sense, neither governments nor couples are proactive and smart enough in appreciating and resolving the true problems of relationships.

Generally, couples' zeal for individualism, pushed by their varied idiosyncrasies, makes them competitive and vengeful. Their prides hinder their sense of compromise regarding their fanciful expectations from marriage. These are essential facts couples ignore at the beginning of a relationship. Their naivety about the potential niceties of relationships dulls their senses about people's inherent greediness and growing obsession with independence and self-gratification. They are careless initially, as they rely on courts to make up for their lack of practicality and sincerity at the outset.

For clarity, now let us look at this picture from the opposite angle: Let us assume courts would rule only on limited, crucial arguments raised in marriages. Under this condition, suddenly partners recognize the need to be more proactive and blunt at the outset. They will try to find ways of protecting themselves in case their relationship fails. They would now really exercise their authority as independent individuals and write a *contract* in line with their marital expectations and the settlement terms in case of separation. This approach and mentality have many merits that will be explained in the upcoming pages. However, its main goal is to stress on partners' independence in setting a viable marital atmosphere compatible with their personalities, aspirations, and needs according to some logical principles. Whether their decisions are perfect or flawed is irrelevant, as they make them as two independent individuals. Of course, couples can always depend on expert advice to prepare the right contract for their needs. In fact, as new mechanisms and *relationship models* are developed and become available, many standard documents would be out there for couples to use for choosing a proper relationship model and the type of contract that best suits their needs. We are not still addressing the mechanisms, which will be elaborated later. Here we are merely trying to examine the concept.

Limiting government's role in relationship decisions would empower couples' drive for independence, as the responsibility of taking care of their personal interests is left to them. They grasp and use a proper sense of individualism, instead of using it just for hiding their insecurities the way it is customary now. They study the potential risks and likely scenarios in modern marriages along with their needs and expectations in advance. This exercise makes them more careful at the outset and less frustrated at the end when separation feels imminent. This is what people want and should get. It is time for governments to treat people like mature, independent citizens to a great extent. This process would also make couples more open and sincere about their needs. They would realize the potential risks of making their marital decisions without ample planning or too emotionally before and after the wedding. They take charge of their own fate and become wiser. And those who only pretend to be independent must finally learn to become one and state their needs clearly, instead of only making so much noise later!

2. **Support and participate in all kinds of research to enhance the quality of a universal 'relationship framework' and principles for the new era.**

All the money governments and legal systems could save by minimizing their direct roles with relationships' and partners' conflicts can be spent on supporting universities and scholars to refine the relationship framework and GARP. Governments can also find ways of controlling consumerism that is goading people to overextend themselves financially, which is a major source of family quarrels and collapse. Instead, they should teach family budgeting and the relationship framework at high schools and colleges very seriously. Governments have a big responsibility to protect their citizens against the evils of greed and neediness that are overwhelming all aspects of social life. Obviously, this is a lot of expectation by this naïve author in a civilization ruled by conglomerates and a bunch of hypocrite, greedy, incompetent leaders! However, it is necessary to admit to at least the sources of our problems and human sufferings.

For one thing, people seem to have lost their senses about the level of debt they should carry. They are lured into credit shopping, while governments ignore the spread of unethical business practices ruining families and leading to economic instability. People cannot curb their temptations and reduce their excessive expectations. They cannot stop competing with friends and families for buying a house or other stuff before their jobs and incomes are secure for their reckless spending. Most people do not have the willpower or financial sense to stay away from *ridiculously prevalent* marketing gimmicks. In all, the level of financial risks that people take does not fit their particular financial situation. And allowing capitalism exploit people's weaknesses is governments' utter disregard for social welfare. Letting consumerism push couples into despair and separation is a crime. It is a good indication of governments' absolute failure. Governments' role to push consumerism to boost the economy is coming at the cost of family destructions and imminent social catastrophe. They must change their own mentality and then teach life's reality to people, too, instead of letting the existing financial chaos get even more out of hand. They should also become a lot more conscientious and active in teaching people how to budget and live within their means. *Then again, these ideals merely reveal this author's endless naiveté and optimism!*

In the past, couples depended on religions and cultures to define and regulate relationships according to some ethical guidelines. Now that those modes are no longer functional, it is vital that governments play a more prominent role in two fronts: **First,** minimize its interference with the *symptoms* of relationship failures. (This would make partners more vigilant about the purposes and potentials of relationships and more proactive to find solutions.) **Second,** promote the guidelines of the 'relationship framework' as a fundamental social norm for couples to follow. Governments should no longer subject the fate and health of society to couples' arbitrary approaches, or assume relationships can thrive without a plausible framework.

3. Support and teach the modern 'relationship framework' to the public in detail, especially at high schools.

Once governments, universities, and scholars come on board and agree about the need for a modern relationship framework, they should support its development and propagation actively. Most important of all, the relationship framework, models, needs, and mechanisms must be taught in high schools and colleges, with strict rules for passing these mandatory courses. They are more important than sex education.

Maximizing the public's welfare and social health are the main goals of any government. As such, it has a responsibility to support a type of relationship framework that corresponds with both social conditions and partners' companionship needs effectively and efficiently. Government should not leave this important task to chance and hope that things would work out nicely on their own in society ultimately.

Again, it should be stressed that family budgeting and debt management are integral parts of the 'relationship framework' for keeping families together. While both governments and people should remain vigilant about family finances, grasping the cause of this turmoil and teaching them to the public and youths is governments' and universities' role.

Another kind of government support is to give newlywed couples access to free counselling, especially during the first year. The idea is to monitor their knowledge and practice of GARP. This process can keep them on track and stop their unreasonable demands building up. The process is something like giving a learning permit to couples, while they are trying to get the hang of their relationships and before problems pile up and get out of control. Couples should use the counselling service to learn about choosing a proper relationship model, building their relationships, and preventing marital alienation, so that they spend much less time on problem solving. We need a preventative approach.

Chapter Eight, suggested a model for creating a primary balance between personal needs and the relationships needs. The importance of developing this balance and choosing the corresponding relationship model were discussed accordingly. Relationship models and success factors are good tools for both relationship planning and contract preparation. They are all topics that should be taught in high schools and during the counselling sessions.

4. Support and Propagate the concept of R-entity—the idea of perceiving marriages as an independent entity like a business enterprise.

Governments and scholars should devise the mechanisms to view marriages as a business enterprise—R-entity. Especially, they should require partners to sign a basic contract before a marriage certificate is issued. This would facilitate partners' acceptance of the new approach and the implementation of the new social mentality. It would reduce the current burden on legal systems largely, too, while couples learn about their roles to protect themselves personally as independent individuals.

Just imagine if business partnerships and corporations were created without contracts to delineate shareholders' rights and equity arrangements at the outset. It would have looked quite ridiculous and extremely expensive to deal with all the claims that partners and shareholders would have wanted to settle in courts. It would have also looked ridiculous if shareholders or business partners had to go to court to ask for a permission to terminate their businesses or partnerships. The idea of settling relationship issues in courts at its current extent (especially financial ones) is just as ridiculous, especially considering that more than 60% of people in modern societies would have to go through separation and divorce with some kinds of claims to settle. Some people must endure this stressful process more than once, as multiple marriages have become common for many of us. A contract is a must for starting relationships now.

5. Support and teach the idea of time-bounded marriages in legal channels, while limiting government's role in financial and custodial decisions.

'Longevity' has traditionally been an excellent indicator of a successful relationship. The religious teachings, tradition, and psychological benefits of a stable relationship have had a lot to do with this mentality. Naturally, the longevity of relationships has many advantages if it could be mastered properly. Three questions must be answered, though:

a) Are humans instinctively equipped to live together for the length of their long lives (especially with life-expectancy growing so much)?
b) Do partners' personalities and needs support the possibility of living together forever?
c) Do our new social values and settings induce the longevity of relationships?

The rather lengthy discussions in the next section regarding the above three questions will offer a resounding answer 'NO' to all these questions. So, for helping relationships, our social mechanisms must be revolutionized in order to match the new social needs and people's evolving characteristics, especially their increasing needs and arrogance. How? Well, we could eliminate the need for a marriage certificate and registration. This way partners can get in and out of their relationships as they wish, like the way nature has meant this basic human urge to work. However, since we are social beings in need of rules and statistics, we should find a compromise. Having a basic social order to register our *marriage contracts* has some advantages, too. However, the main point is to make 'marriage contract' a prerequisite for registering all marriages.

A major discussion about the format and conditions of marriage contracts would be necessary in some other place or book. Nevertheless, a marriage contract must specify all the financial and non-financial terms agreed between partners and then specify *a term* (like five or ten or fifteen years) for the relationship, too. Setting a specific term for a relationship feels too radical for many people, obviously. However, it has many advantages as explained later in this chapter under the heading of 'reverse psychology.' After this initial period, partners may renew the contract for another term, with or without changes to other clauses. Or they could simply let the contract expire, which means their marriage ends automatically without a need to burden the court system or cause partners' undue stress.

Inserting a term for relationships fits within the progressive relationship framework quite nicely. It helps partners develop a new mentality that matches their needs for individuality and making decisions with the least amount of hassle and stress. The psychological impact and benefits of including a 'term' in our marriage contracts will be tremendous, in the author's opinion. First of all, it sets partners' mindsets properly when they start their relationship. They extend more efforts to learn about, i) relationship needs, ii) the realistic expectations from their relationship based on the terms of their marriage contract, and iii) the relationship model they choose for themselves. They prepare themselves for a relationship that would be quite fragile (and temporary) unless they show serious interest in keeping it. Thus, the reality about the inherent vulnerability of relationships, nowadays, is truly felt and respected. It would also eliminate the artificial needs or motives for getting into a relationship. And most important of all, partners respect their partners and their relationship (as R-entity), because at the end of the term they are no longer bound to stay together. The child custody and all other aspects of relationships are worked out in the contract as well. Standard contracts would become available and considered an ordinary process for everybody to adopt. It would no longer be unromantic to sign a contract—because it would be a prerequisite for all marriages. The only thing partners must do is to make their desired adjustments to a standard contract, jot down the terms, and then sign it. And the only thing the government should do, if this process is supported, is to ensure contracts are prepared as a requirement. Courts would deal with a small number of legal cases that partners might bring against each other only regarding the execution of their contract terms.

In addition to a fixed term in contracts for the automatic annulment of relationships (unless renewed), contracts could also include optional clauses for separation or terminating a relationship before its formal deadline based on pre-specified conditions and subject to a prior notice of let us say a few months or one year by one (or both) partners.

Another radical step that partners should adopt in line with a time-bounded marriage is to celebrate their relationships at the end of each successful term, instead of doing it so lavishly at the beginning when there is so little guarantee for partners' abilities to relate to one another successfully. Stop wasting too much effort and money on some event before it is established that partners really deserve to celebrate their abilities to cohabit harmoniously. It is very likely that they are going through this whole shenanigan called wedding vainly based on their naïve image of relationships the way it is universally misperceived, nowadays. It is amazing that, after decades of trials and errors with marital rituals, we do not stop to question our wisdom about the purpose of it all if we still cannot cohabit civilly!!

6. Limit government's role in financial and custodial decisions.

In line with the points raised above about supporting people's urge for individualism and independence, all social units and systems, including scholars, universities, and the public should propagate and push to limit governments' role in regulating, and ruling about, relationship affairs. The more they stay out of this affair, the more and sooner couples will learn to depend on themselves and teamwork to manage their contracts' terms. They learn cooperation and tolerance. They start to act like mature, thinking creatures that humans are supposed to be. All likely conflicts arising from relationships should be dealt with based on partners' contract as much as possible.

The biggest benefit of limiting governments' role is that couples become proactive and cautious about their marriages. This approach would change people's mindsets and attitudes. There will be less unfit relationships and couples stay together longer, simply because they have thought through relationship stages at the outset realistically, especially the heartbreaking ending that a majority of relationships faces, nowadays. They enter their relationship with prepared, practical mindsets and cooperate harder to make it go beyond the initial term.

Surely, this radical suggestion is exactly opposite to what has been advocated in the recent decades where governments have felt obliged to interfere in people's relationships in hopes of protecting their rights and enforcing some marital order and fairness. In reality, however, this scheme has damaged family relationships and people's senses about getting in and out of their marriages quite sloppily. People have become lazy! They neither understand and observe new relationship requirements, nor spend enough time to establish their rights and needs in the case of separation, which is the most likely scenario these days. In general, partners can resolve their conflicts through:

i) love and trust, ii) logic and compromise,
iii) courts, iv) contract,
v) contract, plus a combination of the above methods.

Obviously, partners cannot rely on options (i) and (ii) above to solve their conflicts or finalize their separation. It would be a waste of paper to explain why, although most reasons can be found in this book already. Therefore, nowadays, couples wait until their relationship feel terminal and then resort to courts to make all the financial and emotional decisions for them. Yet, if they just had a contract to set the boundaries at the outset, they could not only resolve their conflicts without hassle, but indeed take routine actions to avoid conflicts and prolong their relationship naturally. Option (v) appears like the ideal (most optimistic) method, as it relies mostly on a contract, but might utilize partners' love and logic as well. The bottomline is that a contract is necessary in the new era for couples to manage their marriages, so it must become mandatory. That is, courts should minimize their role in mediation and resolving marital issues.

Many aspects of a binding relationship can be planned in advance efficiently in a contract. The major role of a contract is to bring full transparency into relationships, especially about common contentious issues, nowadays. Another big benefit of a contract is that the ambiguity and uncertainties of the present setting would be resolved largely. Those people who count on courts' mercy to exploit their spouses would be eliminated from the path of corrupting relationships and ruining the social mentality in general. Standard contract forms can provide a variety of options for couples to choose from and to address their special needs easily. For example, the matter of child custody and support can be agreed upon at the outset by choosing one of several options predefined and explained in standard contracts. Couples could agree on joint custody or one partner taking the full custody of children after separation, with certain visitation rights.

The matter of child custody and child support could be also linked or not. For example, in one option, the parent taking the custody would be responsible for all or most of the expenses. It might appear reasonable to some couples that the partner *getting the honour* of raising a *snotty* kid should pay for its expenses, too. Still, many other options exist, of course, to choose from based on couples' preferences. The child support amount would be easy to set up at the outset, too, in case the contract stipulates that one partner should pay child support to the other. It may be based on a percentage of the government's child support rate every year, which is set at a reasonable cost of living index. For example, a couple may agree that it should be at 200% or 80% of the government announced rate for the years subsequent to their separation. For these cases, if the government rate is $500 a month, the partner paying the child support would be paying $1,000 or $400 a month (i.e., 200% or 80% rates respectively). To be honest, the author cannot see why some kids should be spoiled more than average children in a modern society. Why should wealth have anything to do with child support money? These symptoms are all part of our crooked social values when we assume that some kids should be spoiled more than others because of their parents' wealth. Nonetheless, setting child support at a fair percentage of the government rate would take care of this matter, anyway. Some couples might wish to negotiate at the outset to set the child support at ten or fifty times the government rate, if they really want to. Whatever! The whole point is to be clear about it at the beginning. All of these terms must be stipulated clearly in the initial contract or through future modifications made to the contract only by mutual agreement. No judge should have a right to override these contracts, either.

By the way, the concept of couples signing a relationship contract is not new or unromantic. For many centuries, a form of contract has helped couples stipulate their expectations and boundaries according to cultures and religions. Only in new cultures a preference for ambiguity has found ground, because signing a contract seems unromantic, and also because a large group of people benefit from this ambiguity.

The matter of alimony follows the same logic. That is, couples must agree initially if alimony is necessary at all. With all the push for independence, nowadays, one partner paying alimony to the other sounds hypocritical. Still, it would be easy to include a formula also for alimony, as a percentage of the government rate for a reasonable alimony in line with the cost of living—if quite necessary and partners are old-fashioned with no sense for independence and pride!

Decisions about having kids at all and whether one partner should carry a higher role for raising them are getting more sensitive, nowadays, too. Although many couples use nannies, still emphasis on one's career might cause arguments between spouses. One way to settle this matter is to make the partner who insists on having children accept the main role in raising them, while the other partner's role and degree of involvement are also negotiated in advance and recorded in their marriage contract. Definitely, the question of having kids at all would become even more contentious in the future. Partners should decide carefully whether they are ready and capable of raising kids for living in tough societies, and how they would be able to prevent spoiling them with vain values and materialism.

Sometime in the far future, people might even be given a right to sue their parents for bringing them into this chaotic world or for their way of raising them. This would be a good scheme for making people more responsible for creating kids as an old-fashioned, selfish means of satisfying their maternal urges, *or merely as a hobby!* Why should kids suffer in this crazy world—in dysfunctional families, corrupt societies and polluted environments? Bearing children should become a calculated decision by intelligent parents rather than a careless or selfish act to enrich their own lives; it should not be even for socioeconomic purposes of governments. We should think more about the creatures who must face the social chaos, not their parents' happiness or even manpower needs. The closer we sense the fate of humanity, the fewer kids we will create!

Maybe some time in the future we get to a point where parents would be required to pass certain tests in order to get a permit for bearing and raising children! That might be a more acceptable responsibility for governments in terms of people's marital affairs. Naturally, these measures sound inhumane, but rather urgent for a desperate civilization like ours to remain functional. On the other hand, if humans are supposed to be intelligent, but still keep causing pain for themselves and their children, maybe we need a more ethical standard of behaviour as well, even about bearing and raising children.

7. Support and propagate the idea of partners' financial autonomy and responsibility with only minimal reliance on court systems.

The above six adjustments in social mechanisms show that diluting the government role in relationships would have the highest effect on the financial independence of partners. Every marriage has its unique characteristics and financial demands, so it should have a specific budgetary format that best fits its partners' needs, too. It is also wise to discuss, or perhaps even document, this budgetary format at the outset. Of course, each couple can adopt one of the standard formats suitable for most relationships. When available, these formats will be flexible to suit most families with special budgetary needs, while overall partners contribute to household budget based on their income. The formats also accommodate the circumstances when one partner is not working, temporarily or permanently. However, beyond their routine contributions to the general family budget, partners handle the rest of their income as they wish. They make their money and invest independently, choose to invest together, or share information about their investments if they wish. Yet, the old mechanism about partners' meddling in, or knowing about, each other's financial affairs is not practical or sensible now. Withholding information about one's income or investments would not be considered rude or illegal.

Partners' current sense of entitlement to know everything is quite absurd in the world everybody advocates independence and equality. The purpose of agreeing on the financial format, possibly in writing, is not to be secretive or uncompassionate.

Rather, the point is to mitigate the effects of the contentious areas of conflict between partners. This goal fits nicely within the relationship framework's overall objectives.

Modifications of governments' legal responsibility towards relationships will impact partners' financial independence the most. Instead of courts deciding regarding the distribution of assets at the time of separation, partners should agree at the outset, independently and objectively, on a system fitting their expectations. Most marital quarrels are about financial issues, as partners' demands at the time of separation are so different from what they had expected (or expressed) at the outset.

Minimizing financial arguments by agreeing on some basic financial responsibilities—mostly through a contract perhaps —forces partners to concentrate on teamwork, the welfare of the family, and keeping a viable family budget, which includes all the facets of their lives, including long-term financial needs and obligations of the family. Then, what each partner does with his/her money outside their family budget is essentially his/her business.

Again, it should be emphasized that the main point of these seemingly cold and absurd financial formalities is to eliminate the hassles and repercussions of current relationship conflicts caused by financial mechanisms. Partners' constant nagging or retaliation, nowadays, as customary attempts to control each other's financial affairs, is causing too much misperceptions and arguments beyond the scope of this book's discussions. All these contentions points would be resolved systematically when practical martial contracts make life and relationships easier for rational couples.

Main Questions about Relationships Longevity

Some elaboration with regard to the prospects of relationships longevity in new relationships would be useful by dissecting the three following questions:

a) Are humans instinctively equipped to cohabit for the length of their long lives (especially with life-expectancy growing so much)?
b) Do partners' personalities and needs support the possibility of living together forever?
c) Do our new social values and settings induce the longevity of relationships?

(a) In terms of the role of instincts, the discussions in Chapter Two, especially 'The Effect of Human Hormones,' provided a resounding answer 'No': Humans are not innately equipped to cohabit permanently. The simple fact that we all have this doubt (regarding humans' instinctual capacity to be monogamous) answers the question largely, too. It means that, at best, we are not quite sure! In fact, we witness how liberally humans commit adultery left and right these days. They just cannot tame their sexual desires and adventurous mentalities. By definition, any instinct is absolutely explicit, permanent, collective, and it requires no deliberation regarding its nature. The innate monogamy and devotion among some creatures, e.g., crows or penguins, demonstrate the meaning of instinct. Playing those roles is their true nature. They do not have to argue and fight over their gender roles, equality, or infidelity, either. They know and accept their roles naturally and they are not so eager to change them the way we humans do. Like, for example, a lioness suddenly insisting that it is tired of doing all the killing and that this duty should be shared from now on or that male lions ought to do it. Humans clearly lack these types of instincts, and instead keep arguing about their *new* roles, equality, and infidelity. Thus, the idea of monogamy or devotion must have come as part of social ethics (especially in the older times), or for dealing with our psychological needs and deprivations.

Like most creatures, we humans instinctually prefer our autonomy and sense of adventure, especially sexuality. Let us stop pretending otherwise. Our Egos (and the obsession for independence) prevent us from being reliable instinctually. Referring to the discussions regarding gender differences in other books by this author, it is reasonable to believe that some instinctual differences between men and women actually goad them to deflect (or even fight off) each other. Of course, this does not mean that they do not fall in love or try to support each other. However, many of these conditions are tentative or the residues of cultural norms and religions. Overall, humans have to make special efforts to get along, especially opposite sexes.

The urge to experience sex with many partners is in almost all human beings. We stress too much on sex with different partners, somewhat instinctually and partly culturally, as a means of finding happiness. Thus, as humans' endless appetite for sexual freedom seems innate, it is obvious that we are not instinctually programmed to cohabit permanently, as long as we prefer sexual loyalty, too—as another innate or cultural tendency. Ironically, we are normally also jealous and detest our partners' sexual relations with others, anyway. *We humans are truly too confused and complex—either instinctually or culturally! Perhaps both!*

A cute *relationship* instinct is that men usually try to avoid commitment while women want to lure them into it. Is this a by-product of the women's instinctual need for procreation? Probably not, because women and men of all ages have these urges. Is this really an instinctual urge or only a 'condition' developed because of people's marital experiences throughout the history of mankind? It is hard to say, except for the fact that women seek dependency more naturally than men do, especially during maternity. On the other hand, both genders' growing resistance, nowadays, towards commitment will most likely become even more prevalent in the future as men find it harder every day to respond to, or bear, women's newer needs and demands, and women find men less and less tolerable.

With mistrust rising so fast, the future of relationships seems doomed.

We have accepted the theory of evolution that connects humans to primates and other creatures in general. In the great kingdom of God, the primary role of the male and the female is to reproduce (sexual urge). Their secondary role is to protect one another against adversaries and harsh environments. In particular, the role of the females in protecting and upbringing their offspring is prominent. Males are usually less attached to the offspring, and even towards the females, once the initial mating process is complete. Often the females play a major role in cooling off the relationship, too, especially after the offspring gets strong. The males merely obey by keeping their distance or moving away altogether. Humans are seemingly driven by similar instincts, despite the social norms devised to keep them together, focused, and tactful. The evidence for such instincts in humans is not hard to find. We know that:

- Women are more eager to procreate. Their biological clock goads them to get this matter resolved as soon as possible. Women also have a higher urge for maternity. Thus, they are more anxious to find a suitable man and lure him in for the ultimate objective of creating children. Although the women's innate need for reproduction seems to rival their career goals, nowadays, their ambitions are mostly superficial, as explained below. Deep down, they are more attached to, and protective of, their children than men are. Actually, their inherent need for reproduction is more important to them than their urge for independence or career, unlike men. Yet, women's higher urge and urgency for procreation also induce their higher need for dependency on men during maternity at least.
- Women show less interest in their husbands when children begin to satiate their emotional needs. Often, their children become more important to them than their husbands. Thus, their urge and courage for independence rise when the main objective of nature (reproduction) is fulfilled. Of course, if

husbands happen to lose their interest or their focus during this confusing process (game), women eventually look for another mate to satisfy their inherent dependency needs and passion.

- Both genders, but mostly men, are lured by other people's charm once their initial attraction to their spouses wears off. Especially, when people age, they crave the company of younger people. They feel vibrant and young when they get the attention of the opposite sex and often believe they can revive their youth by pursuing new adventures, instead of bearing the same life routines with an old, nagging spouse. All of us have this vile weakness—perhaps a natural way of responding to our psychological need for adventure and fear of aging. The fact that some people do not act upon this natural feeling, due to their ethics, fear, or integrity does not change the main principle about people's natural tendency to experience love and sex with someone else other than their spouses.
- People resent monotony and get depressed if new adventures are not instilled in their lives rather regularly. Living with the same partner often becomes too monotonous.

So, people are not mentally (or instinctually) built to tolerate monogamy for many years, especially in a society like ours that stresses on pleasure and making the best use of our lives.

(b) In terms of partners' personal defects, needs, and misperceptions, the chance of partners tolerating one another for a long time is constantly decreasing as personal stress and defects increase in society. As discussed, mostly in Part I, with our personal needs increasing in the new era, we have become more arrogant and built a sense of entitlement. Accordingly, our dogged Egos prevent us from understanding one another and relating. The trend demonstrates that our personal needs are rising constantly and we value our independence more than anything else, nowadays. More independence and emphasis on self-gratification lead to relationships' lower longevity. The urge for maternity could decline, too, as women stress more on their need for independence, sexuality, and careers.

Overall, people's obsession for pleasure, adventure, and love obviously makes them too restless, thus reduces their sense of commitment in relationships. This newly emerged mentality for people is affecting their perception of life and their relationships. They live longer and want to spend it with people who can give them more pleasure than their existing partners. So they move out of their boring relationships much quicker than it would have probably made sense even a few decades ago.

The variety of games that couples play, nowadays, in their relationships for various reasons is also getting more bizarre and destructive every day. People's idiosyncrasies and shallow needs are making their games complex and unmanageable for couples. Few people know how to behave and relate to one another naturally in the new world.

All these growing barriers in relationships impede the chances of longevity.

(c) In terms of social settings' impact on relationship longevity, the origin of 'lifelong relationship' ideology must be explored in religious and morality ideals of many centuries ago that we no longer advocate. Instead, in modern societies, we have new principles, mainly guided by partners' needs for pleasure, individualism, and freedom. While the author highly advocates relationship longevity, the matter must be tackled realistically based on the new rules, which will be explained shortly. The bottomline is that the present social structure and values cannot teach people to cooperate in their relationships. Rather, it mostly promotes individualism, which then raises family conflicts. Chapters One and Four explain the reasons longevity can no longer be a realistic expectation that couples can satisfy in their modern relationships. The old social tenet for longevity is against our instinctual propensity and it does not fit our new lifestyles, mentality, and the new demands of relationships.

Overall, the assumption that humans can learn to get along has so far proven quite inaccurate. On the contrary, humans are probably worse than most creatures in terms of learning about existence to relate easier. Animals at least do not kill their own kinds for so many silly justifications that humans offer. We do not hesitate to destroy each other ruthlessly. We have killed over hundred million of our kind so casually in the last century alone, by far the largest number in human history. Apparently, the more civilized we allegedly become, the more ferocious and greedier we get. We have the United Nations and we have all these charitable organizations and generous people, but more people are dying every day in wars, from diseases, and from hunger. Worst of all, the so-called civilized nations and their leaders are only pursuing their own interests, especially for gathering more wealth and power, regardless of the chaos they are creating around the world. Heck, the whole meaning and sense of democracy and decency has been in a big jam for a long time already.

In addition to the egotistical nature of all humans, male and female seem to have even a harder time to grasp each other and get along. People are not made or trained to be in civil relationships. Especially nowadays, they are brought up too pompous, while focusing on finding happiness, too! To them, companionship is only another means of capturing that elusive happiness; or reversely, a mere obstacle for finding happiness. People no longer recognize or admit that life's hardships and relationships' agonies do not vanish regardless of their naïve expectations and shoddy slogans.

So, what chance the concept of relationship longevity could have in this environment?

The Magic of Reverse Psychology

The merits of having a term specified in relationship contracts are substantial. In particular, the reverse psychology works perfectly in this special case, mostly for prolonging marriage relationship. Just to mention a few points, it will:

1. Change the entire social mentality about relationships.
2. Guarantee partners' increasing needs for individualism and independence.
3. Satisfy the instinctual urges of humans (for companionship and procreation) without unnecessary formalities.
4. Free partners from feeling trapped.
5. Keep partners hopeful about future and happiness if their present relationship fails.
6. Make partners smarter about life and their decisions related to binding relationships.
7. Raise partners' interest to learn and practice the 'relationship framework' and GARP.
8. Introduce a progressive and proactive mindset for partners.
9. Increase love and cooperation in relationships.
10. Enforce teamwork with a more crucial role in relationships.
11. Increase longevity of relationships.
12. Make children's lives less stressful and more predictable.
13. Reduce stress in families and society as a whole.
14. Reduce the sense of possessiveness and jealousy.
15. Reduce the burden on court systems substantially.
16. Eliminate the need for couples to spend outrageous legal fees.
17. Reduce the fear of getting into relationships and facing its hassles.
18. Raise economic productivity and social welfare due to lower stress and time wasted on relationship retaliations and wars between partners and in courts.

It will take a rather long time before social mechanisms are in place to accommodate relationships' new needs. However, we can think and behave more objectively now personally, as though these new values and mechanisms were in place. We can do so by learning how to live more independently, write a marriage contract, and get out of our marriages civilly, when necessary, without being so vengeful and greedy.

Epilogue

We all have felt the daunting complexity of relationships in the new era. The relationship concepts discussed in this book and the suggestions for radical remedies also provide a good perspective of social mayhem and our sufferings. Accordingly, readers may find an incentive to explore their relationships a bit more methodically and patiently now. They can read the other books in these series to get even more insights about the depth of relationship conundrums. They, especially concerned scholars, might also contact the author to offer their feedback and perhaps state some major clarifications if they wish.

Obviously, making all the mental adjustments suggested for improving our relationships and agreeing with the needed radical solutions would not be easy for any of us. However, if we really wish to have an effective relationships environment, we should get serious and maybe even read this book again to ponder the points more deeply this time to realize that:

- Relationships have very specific needs of their own, which are different from couples' personal needs.
- Acknowledging and satisfying relationship needs diligently are necessary for keeping partners alert and objective, and for boosting the health of their marriages. These needs were listed at the end of Chapter Four.
- Relationships are supposed to fulfil certain limited goals for couples. Yet, we have lost our sense regarding these realistic

relationship purposes, and instead placed a lot of demented demand on our relationships. We have created many shallow ideals for ourselves based on our naive urges for love and happiness in relationships. Relationships' realistic purposes were explained in the first five chapters, in particular.

- It is imperative that some form of objectivity and order be brought back into relationships.
- Relationships must be managed according to meaningful principles, like the ones suggested in Chapter Seven.
- The old principles and cultures have been eroded in recent decades and now no guidelines exist to help couples.
- It helps couples to revamp their mentalities vastly to grasp the capacity of relationships and cope with its limitations.
- It is possible for couples to *relate* in our so-called modern relationships in some active or passive ways and still fulfil the authentic relationship purposes.
- Certain relationship models exist that can help couples relate effectively, efficiently, and emotionally.
- All the above steps and ideas must be viewed together and adopted as a 'Relationship Framework' for understanding and monitoring our relationships.

We all crave a reliable, passionate, and mature companion to make our lives complete or at least bearable. However, hardly anybody realizes that without satisfying relationships' specific needs and adopting a proper relationship model, partners can never relate effectively. Without proper mindsets or training about the reality of relationships, nowadays, we lose our soul mates even if we are lucky to find them in the first place. All along, the best we seem able to do is to look for some signs of compatibility as a factor for making our relationships rather successful. Even then, we try to find a so-called compatible or ideal partner according to our fantasies and misleading social norms. Alas, the present methods of measuring compatibility cannot deal with relationship needs and conundrums, anyway.

Even measuring some level of couples' compatibility is still in its crude state. Therefore, couples would continue to fail, even despite their supposed compatibilities, because they do not understand the basics of a relationship framework and do not observe the sensible guidelines for maintaining a relationship.

Obviously, compatibility improves partners' opportunities for communicating and relating to each other. Sharing certain values and having compatible mentalities could bring some objectivity into couples' relationships now. In reality, however, even this basic tool for introducing harmony into relationships is constantly sabotaged by partners. We not only do not know how to measure compatibility, but also ignore the basic signs of incompatibility when they are clearly in front of us. For example, when we are in love or need a companion urgently, we ignore the hassles of incompatibility and relationships in general. It seems as if some evil forces are at work to make us choose the wrong partners for ourselves. Sometimes, we go out of our ways to dismiss compatible partners in favour of incompatible ones. Sometimes, we prefer jerks because they seem to challenge us. This attitude feels most reasonable to us, too, because of the effects of personal insecurities and social pressures that make us jump into relationships prematurely. The initial chemistry that partners feel toward each other often obstructs their objectivity. And quite often, we do not get the chance to be choosy. When someone shows compassion and love, we stop worrying about the consequences of our gross incompatibilities. This is true especially because the hassles of relationships are not felt until we get involved in one. Or we always believe that the next partner or relationship would be different, i.e., it would be manageable and nice!

According to limited (unscientific) findings, the author has developed a cynical hypothesis regarding the sources of many relationship problems. That is, the author believes that people often feel drawn to individuals whom they are not compatible with in any justifiable measure (if we used the relationship success criteria suggested in this book). The hypothesis also stipulates the opposite: Compatible individuals often feel little or no attraction towards one another. Still they have a better chance of building a manageable relationship for themselves compared with the first group, i.e., incompatible lovers.

Nevertheless, we do no benefit even from the limited value of compatibility assessment. Instead, we depend mostly on our intuition, chemistry, and arbitrary values that our parents and society have injected into our lazy minds about relationships' success factors. Sometime in the far future, couples may find access to reliable compatibility tests to assess where they stand and what kind of a relationship, according to what model, they might be able to build together.

In a group therapy session, divorced individuals offered their main reasons for getting into a binding relationship and choosing their ex-spouses. The answers are quite informative.

- Lifestyle change
- To stabilize my life
- To have a home (fight loneliness)
- To have children
- I loved him/her (the most popular answer)
- Mother/father figure
- Out of pity, I felt sorry for her/him

Obviously, when the initial purpose of a relationship is not valid or solid, the chances of bringing objectivity into it would be slim. After a while, couples realize their mistakes and begin to resent their partners and themselves for being dragged into a relationship so incapable of satisfying their needs (including many superficial ones). Other reasons for couples choosing the wrong partners are: physical attraction, lust, social/family pressures, ELove, psychological dysfunction, misperceptions, age, obsessions, material needs, insecurity, loneliness, a lack of meaningful criteria to use, etc.

www.ingramcontent.com/pod-product-compliance
Lightning Source LLC
LaVergne TN
LVHW090938080826
845145LV00003B/801

* 9 7 8 1 9 8 8 3 5 1 0 8 7 *